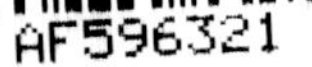

Shadows

Of the setting sun

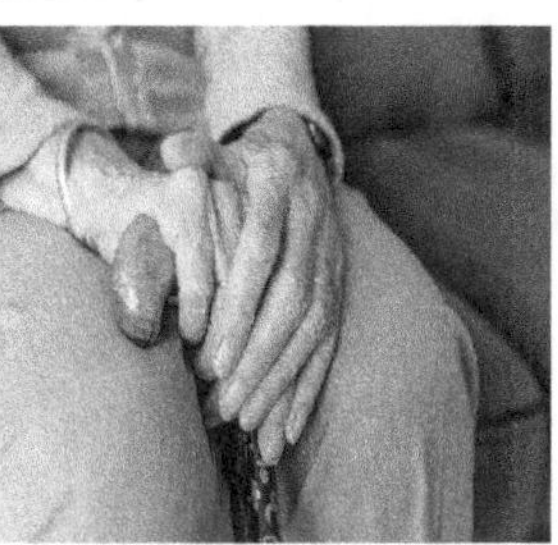

By: Dr. Biplab K Mazumdar

In the colder half of 1997, hundreds and hundreds of people gathered around the maidan to pass the winter in Calcutta, when autumn merged into winter. In a bone-chilling weather, a large contingent of elderly persons got used to having fresh air at morning in the maidan. They're most out on Sundays. The sun appeared like the sun-god at his rising early in the morning, shining like a goldsmith's shop in Cheapside. A cloth or shawl or coat in different sizes had tied over the body of age-old men and women. Misfortune followed them like a faithful hound. The cold wind was sighing in the branches of old trees. A jet was streaking across the sky. The noise of quacking and quarrelling birds and the ruffle of wings made the morning a soothing and monotonous music.

Some age-old men and women of Old People's Homes, slowly bending from the waist and bringing their heads down to their knees, were struggling hard to walk on with their walking sticks of different kinds---bamboo-made walking sticks, twig-made walking sticks, steel-made walking sticks, and other slender sticks. They wrapped closely in winter clothes. A few stray dogs, in all sizes and shapes, went past them. Down through the ages Calcutta has seen many political upheavals and societal changes together with willfully false, deceptive and insincere persons. Humanly speaking, they are humanly inaccurate.

Many an elderly woman---discarded mistress, a woman who had had an illegitimate child, a woman who was divorced or separated from her husband, a forsaken husband, a widow, and a woman was driven out by her sons---were all walking together with their traditional walking sticks. They envisaged the slum as a hotbed of crime. As they looked at the miserable conditions of slum-dwellers, a few women received a sudden check, producing shyness, shame, and a feeling of inferiority. They looked silly and embarrassed, and fondly remembered their first experience as discarded mothers. They were crying out loudly and without restraint under strong impulses of grief in their own room of Old People's Home. There was a brief silence. Leaves were silences around flowers which were their words.

The elderly persons, wizened by age, were walking unsteadily and clumsily from side to side with their walking sticks. The streets were littered with a load of household rubbish. They stood for a few moments talking in undertones with a small group of men. The elderly women were subjected to mental harassment, abuse, and torture at the hands of their sons and daughters-in-law. Their words were barely a breath against their ears. At this age they had no sense of humour at all. They stood for a moment, looking at the stunning display of the sunset below the western horizon.

Most of the Old People's Homes were designated as having different names---'SantiNiketan' (Abode of Peace), 'Santinir' (House of Peace), 'Santinivas' (Home of Peace), and others. Looking at some elderly persons of Old People's Home (SantiNiketan), an old man, not able to stand up straight because of old age and disease, gravely said to his friends: 'A house divided against itself cannot stand. At this age, we have a dim recollection of our long-gone days, and can't differentiate between yesterday and today and tomorrow. All are same to us. Old age is, I think, as cruel as the grave. We have been sighing for days gone by. At this age, none let the old men tremble to win the hand of a woman, unless they win along with it the utmost passion of her heart!'

As soon as they stepped forward, the old man called attention to a surprising woman, aged about 67, sitting and staring heavenward in vacant eyes. The old man said: 'Who's that woman sitting daily at the foot of a banyan tree in the grey first light of the morning?' A hand touched his arm as they passed under the black shadow of a thorn tree, and a voice whispered: 'It is I, brother!'

He caught the old man by the wrist and dragged him swiftly back into the high grass beside the path. With her face cradled in her palm and her eyes wide and questioning like that she looked more than ever like a child.

His friend said in a low voice: 'She gave birth to five children, all of whom died in infancy. She has now become mad. Her husband was careless with money, by temperament happy-go-lucky and gay. The mysterious quality of life

to her is now mingled with dust. Solicitude for her is enmity to herself. She looks tired and strained and that there are shadows under her eyes. Secrets are not narrated loudly. I do not ask for blessings of God, but O God! Save me from wickedness. Every woman likes living life to the full. The news from the outside world, if it could be believed, was not encouraging. An old man's honour in this city is like an egg; if he doesn't hold it properly it falls and breaks. Let's go now.'

He was pleasantly abstracted from immediate reality---the dregs of our society. Both were in dreamy silence.

'Avoid what is written on her forehead by the finger of destiny,' said the old man, looking at the worried-looking woman: 'we cherish a theory that to listen to warnings, or act upon them, is a sign of panic and shows loss of confidence, and we would rather lose our lives any day than be accused of either. O pretty woman, don't step so haughtily, you will lose your youthful pride in time. It is an exasperating trait.'

The old man said that he knew an elderly woman who had never liked children: she had not wanted any of her own, or been in the least disappointed when none had been born to her; she had looked upon it as a blessing. But somewhere, unsuspected by anyone, least of all by herself, there must have lurked an unquenchable spark of the maternal instinct; and now, unexpectedly, it had sprung alight.

At 58, she had taken a child and looked at it with a sudden awestruck and exultant sense of possession. The sense of possession had grown stronger every day. She had even borne the intolerable heat better because the child had not taken any harm from it, but she had waited and panted and prayed for the rains.

'Who is she? Where does she live?' asked his friend, drinking air into his lungs

'Oh Lord! She died two years ago in our Old People's Home at 83. And her son has now become a Bank officer. He carefully and watchfully looked after her

mother,' said the old man, looking at a close-packed group of children giving forth a low continuous blend of sound.

His gestures, his gait, his grizzled beard, his slightest and most indifferent acts, the very fashion of his garments, were odious to the morning walkers' sight. He trembled for the safety of his old age amidst the tremendous number of elderly persons treading a fine line between tradition and innovation.

Negation and despair were etched into his face. Carried away by the grotesque horror of family life, they were getting older and older. Sons were despotic in temper, denying common justice. Their sons had signified their approval and that with a smile. Leaving their valuables in their houses, the age-old parents marched silently through their way. They couldn't sit by and watch their tragedy happen.

He then took a deep audible breath in weariness, and suddenly felt a sharp pain at his knees. His heart was aching for those poor elderly persons hankering after a suitable shelter.

'Well, well,' one of his friends said sharply, fixing his keen glance upon his face with a little sigh of weariness, 'you have already had dialysis. Mind you! You're a kidney patient. Why do you have come for a walk in the morning? You have to get back to SantiNiketan soon.' The old man gave a wisp of smile and said: 'Better to die, for the world is as a gallows set up, constantly troubling and destroying. Look, not at visions, but at realities.

Looking at a middle-aged housewife walking past them, the old man and other friends got puzzled at the face and form of that beauteous lady. For she was very fair and pleasant to look at, and her robes clung sweetly about her supple limbs and budding form. His brow creased with anxiety. Her wayward hair, flowing in a hundred little curls, was bound in with a fillet, and on her feet were sandals fastened with studs of plastic flowers.

Looking at her beauty, the old man, aged about 77, vividly remembered his wife's beauty as the lively housewife who had left him twenty-years ago in her middle age. He tried keeping an image in his memory of his wife. He

muttered: 'her cheeks blushed like a flower, and her dark soft eyes were downcast, as though with modesty, but smiles and dimples trembled about her lips as that middle-aged housewife was going past them. My wife's beauty stuck out a mile. Her beauty smiled in the confinement of the bud, in the heart of a sweet incompleteness. She was very virtuous and holy woman. She left her permanent and ancestral homestead. I'm now living in my own little world of Old People's Home. To meet, to know, to love and then to part, is the sad tale of many a heart. The future belongs to those old persons who believe in the beauty of their dreams. The death of the wife is more devastating than the death of the husband in old age. Peace, ho, be here!' His friend gave his hand and the old man bowed over it and removed himself hurriedly, mopping his brow with a handkerchief and breathing hard.

Various couples passed him, chattering and laughing, but he kept his shoulder turned to them and no one broke in upon his thoughts, and presently they drifted back towards the main road. But he could not tell these white-faced couples this truth.

The old man looked unhappily at the small, tense face. He said: 'Even my son's petty persecutions and burdensome demands exhausted my peace of mind. His insidious questioning finally wormed the truth out of my mind. A painful and persistent affliction plagued my life. As we grow in age, we will go in frustration. We become more miserable. Death comes close and the goal doesn't come—that is what misery is. That is what frightens us. One difficulty creates a new problem that aggravates the original difficulty---a vicious cycle in old age. Oh, damn all my sons! It's my predestined misfortune.' He though savagely.

Aching with sadness, he sighed deeply at the thought. He had visions of his wife getting hopelessly lost.

With the cawing of crows, uttering the raucous natural call, the elderly persons of Old People's Homes had woken up early in the morning to have a fresh air in maidan. Frightened and disgusted from the pandemonium of family chaos, they shrank away from their sons and daughters-in-law and wanted to

shut themselves off from the world. They all looked ill and weary after the cold, restless nights, and greeted each other, uttering words with a cheerful liveliness 'good morning. Have a good day'. Some had chronic indigestion. They had never ever felt that the Old People's Home would have been waiting for them.

They got out of the Old People's Homes in a hurry. The roads choked with traffic. Finding no alternate way, they had to take to a side street---less important street leading off a road. They heard the mournful choruses of barking dogs. A breath of wind rattled a dead and dried cactus leaf. The sun disappeared behind a bank of clouds.

The shutters and balconies of local residents made the streets look almost Europe. The birds flew away as lightly as the wind. A few months ago the dry summer had hurt the land. Morning walkers of a nascent middle class knew the harsh flaming colours of this sun-scorched city, and the heat had been an intolerable burden to them. Nature acted behind the scenes. At this age, most of them were free from unblushing greed. Many old persons had been suffering from nausea with arthritis, blood sugar, and constipation.

Rising temperature and humidity had affected the boarders of Old People's Homes. They had none to look after them. Unfortunately, they had been tricked out of their life savings; and they had felt stupid. Their enthusiasm about life had trickled away for their sons' crafty underhanded ingenuity to deceive their parents. They had ducked of taking care of their parents. Their sons had misspelled and twisted their words. March had been brought with it a steadily rising temperature, dust storms and the monotonous maddening call of the crow cawing continuously from a straight unbranched trunk.

The fog had disappeared. Everything to the grey-haired morning walkers had become blurred by fog. A pale gleam of tempered sunlight fell through the leaves. And on a hot evening, towards the end of the month, a dry wind rattled the dying leaves of the bamboos and neem trees, and a pack of pariah dogs of the city was baying at a sultry yellow moon rising through the hot dusk. They were uttering in deep prolonged tones. Sad birds twittered sleeplessly calling, calling lost companions. Wheelchair had given greater mobility for some elderly

persons to have fresh air in scenically attractive areas. Their inborn love of nature and inbred political disloyalties were deeply rooted.

It was almost mid-April the night was clear and mild, for the hot weather was unusually late that year and it might well have been early March, so green and pleasant were the grass and the flowering trees. It gave the rooms an airing to promote health and fitness. Many elderly persons, wearing respectable clothes, strolled across the wide maidan with brimful of energy.

It was after nine and the tree shadows were shortening on the white dust, while already the heat danced on the open plain so that the city appeared to shimmer and waver in the blinding sunlight as though it were made of molten glass. Some age-old senior citizens, sitting helplessly and hopelessly on the dust-ridden pavement, could feel the pulse and panic of the city swirling about them from the vey dust and beating down upon them in the blinding. They had been driven out by their sons. There was an ominous silence as the morning walkers passed and a menacing mutter that rose at their back and the faces that watched them were avid or insolent or uneasy. Their progress became slower and slower, and then a stone hurtled out of the crowd. It missed them and a senior woman citizen, who screamed shrilly. She was hospitalized where she had had that.

Most of them had grown up with the experience of World War II. The old shibboleths came rolling off their lips. For most of the well-to-do in Calcutta, dinner was also a shibboleth, its hour dividing mankind. History is always silent about the miserable conditions of old persons like the silent 'b' in doubt. A morning walker leaned over and spoke something very quietly to his friend, looking at an attractive, pleasing call girl waiting for someone:

'I'm afraid. Nobody knows what will happen next in our declining years. Past days obscure rather than revolve the problem. Why does one thing come to our mind rather than another? Sons today are fiendishly complicated and immensely unsound towards their parents. They are like magicians who are masters of deception, and resort to trickery to gain their ends. One day they will feel regretful pain and sorrow for their sins and offences. Their repentance will be accompanied by a complete change of character. I have no compunctions about taking back what is mine. Living in Old People's Home is like a sentence of imprisonment for the remainder of a convict's life. It's like a concentration camp to the accursed and unhappy old people.' He said it in his weeping heart. He was then eyeing up all the women morning walkers tired with a dull, listless fatigue.

His friend said, keeping his voice down: 'Yes, you're right. Happiness always lies between unhappiness. Living in Old People's Home is a sign of the times. To pass the remainder of our life in Old People's Home is, I think, the sequence of physical and mental experiences that make up the existence of an individual.' Another friend, standing beside him, voiced complaints:

'What's with you as you're an age-old widower? How are you? You haven't said a word all the morning. What do you say?' said his friend, steadily looking at him.

"It is the personal trauma of every ageing person who has not been living up to his own expectations in his own family from the time of has beans. Mediocre people, like us, are ready to compromise; they have nothing to lose. I have been confined to a wheelchair since I was driven out from my family due to domestic violence on my property. Now I'm in Old People's Home. Old age has allowed me to wallow in my ignorance. Every person in old age is treated as the second citizen of India. Old age is as certain as that the ocean is the meeting-place of all waters. It is better to be alone than in bad company.' His smile melted away all the tensions. He breathed noisily and with difficulty, feeling mortified gnashing his teeth. Rather that continued the argument, other fellow walkers went away.

He said, chewing betel-leaf together with a betel-nut: "the answer of your second question is I'm like a cancer patient. If you ask a cancer patient, he will say: 'I count my days when to die. It seems to be the last day of my dark and cheerless life. If I stay alive today, tomorrow will not spare me." His words sent a chill down his spine, evoking distressing reminders of cancer patients.

'Do you have ever fallen in love?' asked his shaven-headed friend, taking the large view of maidan open to him.

'Why? Don't forget you're not as young as one is,' said he solemnly, laboring under delusion.

His friend got the giggles and said, showing his teeth: ' The love of a woman is like a mushroom---it grows in one night and will serve somewhat pleasantly next morning for breakfast, but afterwards waxes fulsome and unwholesome. What's your opinion about marriage?' He looked at his friend in a vacant eye.

He said in a low voice: 'at this age, I have seen the consequences of many a married life. Truly speaking, marriage is basically an art: how to live and how to die; how to live and enjoy, and how to die and enjoy; how to live gracefully and how to die miserably in old age; how to make your whole life---death included---a celebration. The decisions of sons after marriage are the greatest problems of old parents. If you try to instruct them, they will only humiliate you. We are in old age; we get to feel love is as fair as lotus when the morn kisses it opening petals. I used to read a lot although I don't get much time for books now. Do you understand what I say?' His friend stood facing him as if he was prepared to argue with him. His friend relapsed into silence.

'Rubbish! Marriage and then family, 'he spat out the words in annoyance, 'Family is like a book---the children are the leaves, the parents are the covers that protective beauty gives. At first the pages of the book are blank and purely fair. Save-your-soul-ism and other virtues are at bottom. Most of the women have been deprived of genuineness, naturalness, and simplicity. Truly speaking, I wanted a worldly-wise woman with a philosophy of personal independence. Family life is always arduous. But I-I...'

His friend was speechless for a few seconds and then said: 'Our only consolation is the expectancy of happy life in Old People's Home. Woman being grown has two ills to fear---Death and Marriage; and of this twain is Marriage the viler; for in Death we may find rest, but in Marriage, should it fail us, we

must find hell---the dreadful pit of the glowing flames of the wrath of God. That is our Old People's Home. I was not aware of this moment when I first crossed the threshold of this life. Eleven persons take eleven paths, but one evil person can spoil many people.'

The old man looked blankly at his friend for a long time until his friend felt embarrassed. Raising his head, the old man said: 'At twenty years of age, our will rules; at thirty years of age, our intellect rules; at forty years of age, our judgement rules; and at sixty years of age, our sons rule over our judgments. At this age, I was forced to leave my house with my wife. To hold your head high is very difficult today. Time is life. Yesterday is but today's memory and tomorrow is today's dream.'

All of his friends were rightly proud of his excellent analysis and its results. They felt remorse as the discourse was at great length on the problems of elderly persons. They got shocked as they found a young boy went past them, wisping smoke of cigarette at the corner of his mouth. Judicious parents couldn't use kindness and discipline to their son in equal measure.

Looking at the weather-beaten and worried-looking building of an Old People's Home, he said in grave accent: 'Old People's Home looks as pale and livid as any skull unearthed from a graveyard. After all, life is like soda-water. Childhood, effervescence corked down and wired; manhood some sparkle, more vapidity; old age, empty bottle, cart it away with the rubbish.'

All of his friends huddled together in silent groups, looking at each other. They were very easily frightened about their old age that shadowed their face.

Looking at a widower's sad-looking face, the old man said: 'Ultimately, old age is as black as burnt coal. It is the chronicle of wasted time like a desert waste-land. Death of the mother for a kid and the death of the wife for an old man are the two terrible misfortunes. To think, truly speaking, without learning is dangerous. We are all caught up in a whirling and hellish vortex of old age in the Old People's Home. There is nothing harder to bear than the reverses of fortune. We're tired of age. Death is rest. My biggest journey will end in this Old

People's Home---the net of suspicious circumstances. The Govt. is quite unconcerned about the homeless ageing persons loitering about hither and thither. We're like said birds. Let there be light!'

'Like sad birds! What do you mean?' asked his friend, looking at him with a grave and thoughtful look

'Sad birds always twitter sleeplessly, calling, calling lost companions as friends have flown, like leaves whirled away by the blast,' said he in velvety voice. He seemed to have got playful criticism from his sons that he had not expected. Their aggressive selfishness had shocked him.

He turned off his face, looking at the ingenuous enthusiasm of school-going children free from pretension and calculation. Behind him, he heard his friend asking; 'Where is God now? Man dies but his influence remains. It is sometimes hard to see and sometimes not.'

Every one of them looked despair, sorrowful, and frustrated after having left their paternal houses. Their sons had not treated them with generosity and thoughtfulness, and weren't generous with their time to look after their parents. They knew suffering was a permanent human condition. They were looking at each with natural curiosities to make other boarders feel at home, taking their hands with discreet manners. Only their footsteps were inaudible on the grass. As they were strolling across the wide maidan, some school-going students, having the ingenuous enthusiasm of children, were singing a high-pitched buzzing song behind them. There was a morass of traffic jams around the maidan.

The elderly persons had settled snugly in Old People's Home in an inconspicuous manner. Hundreds and thousands of slum-children were nestled all snug in their beds lying on the pavements under the open sky. They were of a cheerful and gregarious disposition and always ready to enter into conversion with fellow travellers upon the road and at the wayside halts.

Suddenly, they heard a noisy confusion, full of bewildering tangle, outside an Old People's Home. They stepped up to the spot to see what was

happening, taking care of their own wallet. They got to know that an age-old widower of Old People's Home had committed suicide. His age was 77. They looked at each other in surprise, wondering at his stupidity. One of them spoke very quietly to others: 'His dearest wish was to see his grandchildren again. He was dead and it was no use wishing him alive again. Some say there's a romantic episode behind this tragedy.'

'What? What happened to him?' said an old man in surprise, steadily looking at him. Others remained sullen. A gloomy mood ushered in by bad news in a depressing morning.

He silently looked at the old man and said in a soft voice: 'Two years ago the widower fell in love with a widow, aged about 73, to make himself feel younger and livelier. His new romance seemed to revitalize the widow in heart and mind. They used to meet at the temple of Feringhee Kalibary to welcome relief from the hustle and bustle of city life. Unfortunately, that widow died at night last week, leaving him alone in the wilderness of Old People's Home. Her death was unbearably painful to his loneliness. So he put himself to death.'

One of his friends was speaking in a voice that was barely a whisper, for only the sibilance of the sound reached his ears. But the whispering voice was quick and urgent, and somehow conveyed an indefinable impression of authority.

The old man said, looking at the gloomily silent crowd: 'Alas! That with falsehood our life has been spent; from the Truth we stood far, in negligence went! Our work is not done and the season has fled. Truly speaking, 'Life in old age is rigidly compartmentalized into loneliness and forbidding morose. We should stay with others so that we're not alone against all worse, slower and more difficult situations. Living in Old People's Home is like the death sentence commuted to life imprisonment in old age---a companion in misfortune. But we are not only our people---we are ourselves, ourselves! No we are not---we are chained together by environment and custom and blood.' All remained silent. He found that he was unable to think clearly and wished that he would never think again.

An elderly man flicked his cigarette end into the water where it went out with a little hiss. The rose and saffron of the sunset had faded, leaving the sky awash with clear green light in which a single star blazed and glittered in lonely splendour. The warm, moonlit stillness of the city was another world which had nothing in common with the turmoil and tensions and restlessness that were part of the daylight hours. He turned back to his contemplation of the stretch of maidan beyond the trees, as though his interest in what lay there had absorbed his attention to the exclusion of all else.

He tried to forget what had happened to him after the death of his wife. He couldn't forgive that type of his sons' behaviour. Looking at the crowds out shopping, he went to a wine cellar to buy a bottle of sparkling wine. Holding the bottle under his armpit, he got back to Santinir. He said to himself: 'My wife wished herself a million miles away. She is dead and it's no use wishing her alive again. After her death, my son achieved my property at excessive coast. I was puzzled over his mysterious motive. I was at first too dumbfounded to reply.' He began weeping with convulsive catching of the breath, sobbing out his grief. He left the maidan unhurried and calm.

But in winter the maidan was a world of brilliant colours and dramatic sunsets. And the elderly persons of Old People's Home were always pulsating with life, vigour and activity amid miserable conditions, worsened by internal causes that reciprocally augmented each other. They had to lead a sheltered life in Old People's Homes— dreamlands of nightmare. Living in unspeakable living conditions were unsubstantial shadows of old age like an untidy manuscript.

His footsteps made no sound on the thick dust that blanketed the ground between the avenue of shade trees, The noise of the city beat about the walls of the Old People's Homes night and day, filling the small, hot, stifling rooms with the sound. Even the nights brought only a diminution of the noise: never silence. Heavy vehicles beat in the crowded mazes of the city, mingling their beat with the uninterrupted barking of pariah dogs, the crying of slum children, and the drunken shouts of revelers getting all emotional support with their

adoring fans. They were walking unsteadily by a tottering building and spitting abusive words out—a tragic mistake of young generation.

A few months later, the Durga puja festival appeared at the doors of Bengal. Having celebrated the resoundingly exhibited intangible cultural heritage of humanity, Durga Puja, with a lot of grandeur and unquenchable submission with artless and unquestioning devotion, the people all over Bengal felt depressed in heart and soul after the immersion. This vibrant festival has had the highly-rewarding traditions, culture, and qualities to the people of Bengal for many decades.

Some elderly persons, being gouty and rheumatic, or perhaps bed-ridden, had never dreamed of making their appearance at the festival. And they had finally appeared in the warm sunshine and gone lazily in a festive mood, holding on their walking sticks or wheel chairs, about what they termed duty, and, at their own leisure and convenience. After an hour, some of them got back to the Old People's Home, coughing and wheezing with difficulty.

They knew 'this highly-rewarding festival comes and goes freely, swiftly living and swiftly dying every year.' But the miserable conditions of elderly persons in Old People's Homes—a last resort to the hopeless and helpless old persons--would always be the same as ever. An unpleasant and heavy sensation sat at their heart. Their mind was dazed, wandering in a mist of memories. Swayed by superstition, most of the elderly persons suffered a lot from ignorance, fear of the unknown, and a false conception of causation.

A spell of biting north wind began blowing beautifully as a result of natural forces. The trees standing upright all around the maidan were swaying in the prevailing wind. The boarders of Old People's Homes wilting under the pressure of cold wind shut the windows and the trapdoors by winding their handles.

That time the communist rule in the name of communism was steamrolling the opposition all over Bengal with a look of steely determination. West Bengal has always been an ethnic alloy of many people. Comrades gave a

conspiratorial look to passers-by with a satanic pride. For decades, mental slavery was the most important pillar of communist rule in West Bengal. Their vicious enthusiasm was infectious. A gang of youths was seen walking down the pavement drinking a tot of whisky in a flagrant breaching of time-honoured laws and traditions of conduct. They got used to flirting one fashionable ism after another.

An elderly person said to his old friends, muttering his breath: 'We live in mental confusion and mental anarchy and seek vaguely for truth and beauty and moral support. They are devouring our country's resources, to be honest. Nature doesn't adorn the human ruin with blossoms of new beauty that have their roots and proper nutriment only in the chinks and crevices of decay. Parades and marches are the very stuff of politics in Calcutta. At this age, the thing in the world we're most afraid of is fear. NO of some people is more esteemed than the YES of others. We resign ourselves to loneliness in Old People's Homes, and suffer loneliness to rob us of the health, the confidence, the belief, and joy.' In his nervousness he stumbled over his words. He frowned with mock harshness

'Hush!—oh, hush!' begged a stout ageing person, pausing to peer anxiously over his shoulder. They will hunt us down like mad jackals. We are having a troublesome time. A communist is as a jackal which rushed prowling through the land, as a grim lion that frequents hidden paths, as a powerful bull with sharpened horns.' He drew a short hissing breath between his teeth.

All were satisfied at his masterly analysis. His eyes were sparkling with anger while speaking loudly and distinctly.

'Wow! Why do we fear in old age?' said one of them in surprise.

Steadily looking at him, he said in muffled tones: 'Please go away. I---I fear I am about to be very unwell. Old age is a continuous adjustment of our internal relations to external relations. We don't want to keep our last days of life in darkness and shadows of Old People's Homes. Throughout the history people have used a series of fears---to protect their insecurity, werewolves, witches, and fear of the unknown. In old age, every elderly person is to fear a crowd, and yet fear solitude, to fear to go unguarded, to fear the very guards himself, and to fear to meet Death. Life, at our death, is only a memory without pain. In the Old People's Home, I am alone as the single cloud on a sunny day. Every seeker starts in will and ends in surrender. Do you understand, my friend?'

His friend smiled at him, but he just looked straight through his friend.

'You can't lump the elderly with the disabled about old age,' said his friend, 'What you say is quite ambiguous to me.' His friend smothered a yawn and shifted uncomfortably in his chair.

He showed a ridiculous display of anger. 'Hear! Hear!' interjected the old man, 'We are old as soon as we think we are. The giants of old age had never been so nervous and scared of death in their old age. The world is indebted to them for their amazing achievements. Crabbed age and youth cannot live together. Youth is nimble, old age is lame. In old age, we live together like a lamp, to the last wink. In old age we see--the less the qualities of individual's dignity and worth and capacity for self-realisation through reason, the more will be the number of mad person.'

He and all other friends nodded their heads in agreement. The memory of their own fatuous action of the bygone days caught in their throat and seemed to choke them. One of them asked: 'How will we get rid of this problem? Is there any way?'

Looking at them, he said in a smiling gesture: 'Cultivate good reading habits, for the books you read shape your future, your happiness, you're thinking, and your entire personality.'

The two slum children, recognizing the old man, moved passionately as they passed, and the old man smiled and bowed. Their voice was gay as the voice of a bird in the dawn of a day on a sunshiny tree. The two orphan children, felt insecure in unstructured circumstances, were pale-cheeked, leggy little creatures whose pallid fragility was a cause of endless anxiety to an unexpected and very welcome gift. The unsophisticated and untutored slum-dwellers had always uttered unstressed syllables.

He thought for a while and responded with enthusiasm: 'I do not shrink from the truth. Truly speaking, when they are deluded and disillusioned under the communist rule, cynicism and confusion then follow. It is impossible to tell them precisely what people are thinking; they have to be judged by their acts. The youth of today has too much to live on, but we haven't enough. Physical pleasures are important rather than spiritual values. A comrade, who is always anxious for his safety, never alters his opinion like standing water, and breeds reptiles in the mind. What a fool they are! Let us pray for their safety. Every comrade has three tasks: sleeping, shouting slogans and quarrelling. Better than a thousand words is one word that brings peace. They don't look at themselves, and so they blame one another.' All others got satisfied as the dialogue sparkled with wit.

The use of the streets of this city compelled gentlemen-like citizens to keep on one side of the street and slum children live on the other. He was a school teacher. He didn't know what's what. After a few moments, he said: 'At this age, I'm still now in masculine virtues of courage and strength. Every slum children may be passed from one person to a great one. I try improving conditions for the many in this outworn society.' He sighed deeply at the thought after having lost his beloved wife and son.

All others, walking together with him, completely fell under his spell. They had the same opinion as he said. He said, looking at them in a steady gaze: 'Let us go early to our respective Old People's Homes. Hurry up---it's too late. You know I'm a spastic patient.'

'Sorry we are too late,' said one of his friends. They all resigned themselves to their providence.

On the way of getting back to Old People's Home, he muttered: 'In old age, an elderly person swore a thing to me on Monday night, which he forswore on Tuesday morning; there's a double tongue; there are two tongues. I desire nothing but the reward of a villain. That elderly person is too cunning to be understood. What's his offence?'

There were more unregistered people than the registered. The self-disciplined age-old people accepted pain, disappointment, and a difficult situation under the communist rule without complaining. They were resolutely impassive even in communist propaganda. As the sun was peeping out from behind the clouds, sad birds twittered sleeplessly calling, calling lost companions. Looking at the dark forbidden sky, they got back to their own respective Old People's Homes in bending and twisting movements with ease. Smoking was forbidden in every Old People's Home. A few moments later, the sun flashed from behind a cloud.

Sunday was the only day when the people could relax. The people were concerned about the holiday; the boarders of Old People's Homes were in a dilemma. Their threshold of boredom was low. They seemed undecided whether to go or stay on Sunday. Even some physically handicapped persons got to maidan on wheelchair to get fresh air in the morning. Some elderly persons cycled up to 2 miles in the morning to keep fit. Morning walkers who were physically fit had a lower risk of heart disease. The elderly persons—walking alone in maidan-- basked in the reflected glory of old days. They got to believe: 'Aerobic exercise is like a two for one: good for their body, great for their mind.'

Some elderly morning walkers—wearing wrinkle-resistant clothes-- were seeking after something where they would get happiness. The way they clung to the belief that fun-filled and pain-free life equaled happiness actually diminished their chances of ever attaining real happiness. But in memoir after memoir, celebrities revealed the unhappiness hidden beneath all their fun: depression, alcoholism, drug addiction, broken marriages, troubled children, and profound loneliness. The cumulative effects of elderly persons' deplorable conditions had produced a succession of similar events all over the society. The elderly women, like wagons, rattled most where nothing was in them. And the

majority of elderly men were treated like animals in their own family---they were frightened of their sons and daughters-in-law.

The elderly women were lost, and began to whimper in Old People's Home as they had no enduring and cooperating social group for common ends. They felt living on their sons was more horrible than slavery. Every day was to them a Sunday morning lie-in. The only fault was to them that they had always run against the stream of current fashion. At this age they had no future, but the call of Death was looming large over them. They looked everything with a blanket of gloom and stared in blank dismay as fear made them pale.

Most of the hopeless and helpless women were sent to the school of abandoned Old People's Homes—full of the usual moans and groans. Some of the boarders with incipient Alzheimer's disease were unable to do what they had always done. They seemed to forgetting a lot. Every boarder of Old People's Home—a remote island from the civic society-- was enrolled in the school of negation and despair where time was the teacher.

The sky beyond the balcony of Old People's Home paled with the dawn, and presently the sun rose, filling the quiet, airless room with harsh light and throwing a curved shadow across the wall. Kusum Kumari Devi had feared that shadow. She rose to her feet, crossing softly to the window. The elaborate façade contrasted strongly with the strictness of the interior. She then closed the heavy shutters against the burning day.

Kusum Kumari Devi, aged about 83, finding the silence obscurely alarming, did her best to keep up some show of conversation. Her hair was tied sternly in a bun. She was emaciated by illness making her feeble. She got a sweet scent emanating from blossoms. It seemed to emit an air of serenity. Yesterday she had sat at her window and wished for a daughter with a skin as white as snow and hair as black as ebony. She spent too much time watching the pictorial representation of a cloud formation. Her mental soundness, rationality, and levelheadedness remained sane even in times of crises as she came to Old People's Home.

She often asserted: 'Day after day, countless people die. Yet people live as though they are never going to die. Every seeker starts in will and ends in surrender. Animals are more agreeable friends than human beings—they ask no questions; they pass no criticisms.' She winnowed out certain inaccuracies of old age in Old People's Home---undesirable and unwanted.

The damp cold and fogs of winters in Bengal had always been a torment to the elderly persons, and of late her age once sturdy frame had to shrink and shrivel. She had contracted a chill that turned to pneumonia, and she had died within five days. The wind was moaning through the trees. She was not very steady on her feet these days. She used to sing with a lively, supple voice in the morning. She sang with a new insight into her own nature and the nature of life, with a passion for intellectual adventure with a meaningful smile.

'The night has a thousand eyes,

And the day but one;

The mind has a thousand eyes,

And the heart but one'

The co-boarders of Old People's Home decided to celebrate her birthday with appropriate rites. Looking at them, Kusum Kumari Devi said soberly, in a flash of wit: 'The birthday reminded her that another year has gone by in nursing daily drudgery, meaningless pursuits and old regrets. I'm getting older, my life on earth is ephemeral and my time is limited. When thousands and thousands of people around the earth are celebrating, singing, dancing, ecstatic, drunk with the divine...with such laughter, sanity and health, with such naturalness and spontaneity, how can there be war?' She began using a needle and thread to stitches her worn-out blouse.

A patient of Alzheimer's disease lived in the upstairs of Old People's Home, wearing a gross mask of dismal squeaks and groans. She was lying on the ground, moaning as she was listening to the moan of the wind. The obese old

woman had always seemed a grotesque figure; but now, suddenly, Kusum Kumari Devi saw her with new eyes: saw the kindness and the shrewd wisdom in the bright eyes that peered out of the fat, wrinkled mask; the firmness and character that lay in those small dark hands; and, all at once, the vanished beauty and charm that had once been possessed by this stout and shapeless old woman who had been driven out by her sons and daughters-in-law. She could feel her face puffing up where her son had hit her that resulted in progressive memory loss and impaired thinking. The medicine made her ankles swell and increase in size. She once asked Kusum Kumari Devi, 'Who are you?' Kusum Kumari Devi closed and opened the eyelids quickly.

When Kusum Kumari Devi said in reply that she was her co-boarder of this building, she began to cry. She often forgot what she had eaten food. She wanted to eat again. What's right was what's left. Kusum Kumari Devi assumed an air of confidence in spite of her dismay, but she assumed an air of cheerfulness about the patient. She pretended that nothing had happened.

They were cold, wet and thoroughly miserable, and remained resentfully silent in their rooms as they had had many wild nights. They looked very grave as they had got into their rooms of Old People's Home. The vast field of maidan was used by local shepherds to graze their cows for forage grass. A crow began to caw and the stillness was broken by a babble of bird-song. A flight of parrots screamed out of trees on their way to the river, and other crows awoke and saluted the dawn.

The elderly persons felt stronger as they chose maidan to walk in the morning and find refreshment for body and mind. They liked to think of themselves as liberals in favour of some political and social changes. Some walkers were too old to walk steadily in maidan—more aesthetic than functional. They had to grip on to the nearby railing with both hands. The wind was winnowing their thin white hair.

Large numbers of age-old mothers and fathers left their sons as the owl seems to have deserted its nest. They, lying on the pavements in tattered clothes, were not acceptable to society and were forcibly driven out by their

sons. It was shameful that none of the sons and daughters had tried to help them. They were liabilities to them. In Old People's Homes, they got to learn discrimination between right and wrong, and disentangled themselves from a painful relationship. It was the regular course of relationships between elderly persons and their near ones. They kept their painful agony secret to avoid causing embarrassment. It was an increasingly dangerous situation to our traditional society. Looking at the grossly-made miserable conditions, the trees all around the Old People's Home seemed to have been creaking and groaning in the wind of a cultural desert.

The sky was bright now, and the day was already breathlessly hot. The tall bamboos that concealed the ruined building, towering to the level of the ruined dome, walled in all but a small part of the roof. The light brightened slowly, turning from the first pallid whisper of dawn to the clear glow that preceded the sunrise, and the silence gave place to familiar sounds; faint and a few at first, but gathering in number and volume.

Many senior-most boarders were waiting for a peaceful death in Old People's Home as other elderly parents easily became socially isolated and were threatened with complete isolation from the families. Last week a senior boarder had died a slow and painful death at dawn. Her sons and relatives had not come to meet her at death. She had got no friends to speak of her agony. In all likelihood, she didn't have intended to associate with the likes of other boarders.

Malina Devi was eighty, but she did not look her age. At this age, she was paying attention to personal grooming. She, keeping her clothes and hair clean, read her friend's letter telling of her brother's death as the windows reflected the bright afternoon sunlight. She was very shaky on her feet. Her cheeks were furrowed and writhen like rain-washed crags. She held her hand in a hard grasp with fingers that were feverishly hot and unsteady, and lifting it to her lips, she kissed it. When she lifted her head at last and looked at her in the moonlight, her cold eyes were cold no longer, but as hot and avid as her mouth had been.

As she felt a light wind coming out from the window, her long grey-hair danced round her like a snake. She took a letter from the table. The letter was written in Bengali and the ink was blotted in places as though the writer had been crying and her tears had fallen upon the paper. She was in a sour face. Not to express her piercing agony to anybody else; she used to sing a lilting song in her small room. She didn't like to compare like with like. She had to leave her house as her family had contemptuously disregarded her wishes. She got to feel that the society was callously neglectful of the old persons lying relatively near to her. Her heart was full of speechless sorrow.

Last night she said to her room-mate in gloomy gesture, breathing shallowly: 'It has been lovely having you here. How lovely to see you! I feel a ghastly loneliness in this Old People's Home. For the Lord our God is holy, I get satisfied with this room, furniture, books and curtains that are worn and homely and friendly to the touch. But sleep refuses come to my ears. Every night, in old age, seems to be longer in never-quenching fire of sleepless night. We have been more sinned against than sinning.'

She couldn't figure out a question: 'How can a person, who loves God, ever be sad? God and depression, I think, cannot live in the same heart.' She retired to bed so as to get up early in the morning.

Malina Devi was awakened in the diamond-bright morning by a scream from Nirupama Devi, whose room gave on to the same verandah, and a moment later Nirupama Devi herself, clad in a pink sari over a nightgown and with her soft fair curls in tangled disarray, appeared in Malina Devi's bedroom in presence of her room-mate.

A man had walked into her room, she announced in trembling tones: 'A man, Malina Devi! He didn't even knock! He just walked in! I thought I should have swooned with fright!'

'What did he want?' enquired Malina Devi. Her voice sounded shaky because of old age.

'Oh, he did not want anything. He brought me tea and fruit. He just put them on a table beside my bed and went out again. Don't laugh, Malina Devi! It is most unkind of you! I was never so frightened in my life!'

'That was only the bearer,' said Malina Devi, continuing to laugh, 'Don't worry. You may go now.' She disappeared having a wheezing sound of cough.

Malina Devi was unhappy with the house and soon began to look upon it as home. She was about to raise her voice at the room-mate but stopped herself. The room-mate had seen her only five hours earlier. After a few minutes, she further said:

'Where the country is divided, the river water is divided, and the land is divided, parents obviously are also divided. As it happens today, the parents have also been invited to get separated from their sons. There is love lost between parents and their sons today. Sons today grieve over loved ones they have lost. Most of the sons and daughters are grossly injudicious and flagrantly obtrusive to their parents. Outstanding is the situation where endurance is called for. Their conspicuously offensive words are openly and extremely objectionable to our mind and heart. That new trouble has dawned on my thickening mental horizon.'

The room-mate said, steadily looking at her: 'How can it be possible?'

'Nothing is impossible in the dictionary of modern society,' said Malina Devi

'For the love of God, tell me what you say! Let my feelings be my guide at this age. Sinners are around us. Man is a chaos, a creative chaos. They make the boundary. He who is abandoned by near ones is dear to remote ones I see in this Old People's Home. Every Old People's Home is an unknown world to the discarded parents. All of our thoughts run into tears like sunshine into tears.' She had to lower her head avoiding her tears.

'Heigh, heigh!' said the room-mate assuredly, looking out the window, 'It is easier and wiser to stay in this Old People's Home that you know and can deal with rather than change to a new situation which may be much worse. The shadows of my life lengthen as my age goes down day by day. My son is handsome, with a devilish charm. He hides everything rather than reveals problems. As I left my home, my daughter-in-law gave a devastating smile at me. I'm happy that you express your feelings. I wake up with a terrible hangover. Life is a mystery to be celebrated, not a riddle to be solved. My advice to you is to allay your fears. God forbid! None should square off against the diseases of old age. Strange to say, we are not free to ask any question, to say what our sons think, and to correct any errors. My son will never ever feel prolonged and insistent self-reproach and mental anguish for past wrongs as thieves untroubled by feelings of remorse.' She remained silent. Malina Devi got to feel that her physical sensation was interpreted in the light of experience.

Malina Devi agreed with her and said: 'You're right. In old age, we have never been free; and even our neighbours have always enslaved us. We're in continual fear of death. My old friends passed away, new friends appear in this Old People's Home. All are friendly and attentive to the needs of other boarders. It's just like the days. An old day passes, a new day arrives. The important thing is to make it meaningful: a meaningful friend—or a meaningful day. I'm always cheerful and not worrying about the last days of my life. I know death is a perennial literary theme.' She looked at her in a gay smile.

The room-mate stooped her head so low as if to steal a ring from a dead woman's finger. Looking at the wall of books, she found that a few number of Hindu deities and religious leaders were penned in all around the walls. She tried to squeeze the truth out of hers. They talked of other things for a space, until at last Malina Devi rose and held out her hand.

Malina Devi listened to her in stony silence. Her encouraging words didn't spur her on. A few seconds later, she raised her eye-brows with an affection of suspicion and said in a toothless grin, 'Yes, you're right. I rise with some trepidation. But unhappiness, depression, fear, rigidity in old age—these are inefficient ways of killing myself. Unkindness may do much. If I want a peaceful, unchanging life, there is only one place to go: my grave. At the age of 83, I'm like a geriatric vehicle. It's not childlike humour from my weak minds. Most of the shadows of this life are caused by our standing in our own sunshine. Clouds come floating into my life, no longer to carry rain or usher storm, but to add colour to my sunset sky. I walk briskly for about 30 minutes three times a week. It would starve off age-related shrinking....'

'Don't say more,' said the room-mate with a respectful tone of voice, holding her palms together. Malina Devi tossed her head angrily as she had tossed sleeplessly last night. She then moved her head with a spirited gesture and said:

'Don't forbid me. Let me express my heart-felt agony. The age of every person resembles a book. And old age are the blank pages. The old persons proceed alone into the waste, like a bold vessel leaving its haven to enter on the trackless field of the ocean. At this age, each and every elderly person has one foot in the grave. I feel like a burnt child that dreads the fire.'

She relapsed into silence and then looked out the window. She watched that their national flag was fluttering proudly in the air near the Maidan. She kept rather aloof from all.

A few minutes later, she broke the silence: 'The agony of Old People's Homes---an outstandingly clear example of the evil and destructive side of human nature--- hardly descends on the crowd. Time hangs heavy on my hands. Even my hair is falling off. Death is instantaneous. Our sons don't know parents are always anxious for them to get on. They descended to the level of personal insults. I think it so. Happiness in today's world has become elusive. But if our problem in old age is critically analysed, happiness can be a permanent fixture of our life. We need not live in Old People's Home. Carry on in life, doing our daily duties like the village girl who carries pots of water on her head travelling miles to reach her home, chatting with her friends without spilling a drop. Her inner concentration is on the water.'

She then struck her hand upon her breast. Her eyes were shining brightly with flashes of light. A smile touched her lips.

The room-mate found that she was staring at the lighted doorway as though she could drag back a tall spare figure by an effort of will, and that there was an uncomfortable constriction in her throat.

After a while the room-mate said quietly, 'The elderly persons had sincerely expected, their nightmarish living conditions would have been changed after independence. But it has turned into a frightening dream. A feeling of anxiety haunts them every day. Every government should be convicted of an offense bringing infamy upon the elderly persons. Is it not to be an indispensable obligation to a son to look after his elderly parents? What do you think?'

She gave a slight shrug of her shoulders and said nothing further. Her fear turned into unreasoning panic. She didn't wish to discuss it further. Old age was often regarded in India as being possessed of devils or favoured by God. A mood of melancholy descended on her. She glanced uneasily over her shoulder as though to make sure that there could be no third person near them.

'It's really so. So far as I know there is a risk of dementia as the years roll by in old age. How do we discriminate against a particular age-group and especially the elderly? The simpler a thing, the more difficult it is to understand. I can't understand why are you moaning and groaning all day long? Old age is eating away my self-confidence bit by bit. Are you gripped by a feeling of gripping misfortune? Do you know how to be happy in old age?' said the room-mate, behaving in an excessively humble way.

'Why?' asked Malina Devi inquisitively with a sideways glance. She felt the air moved a little faster and became a light wind. A few seconds later, Malina Devi said in an undertone: 'To be happy in old age is very simple. To be simple is very difficult. At this age, my symptoms include nausea and dizziness. Do you know I wake up in the middle of a ghastly nightmare of death? After all, a person is a product of his deeds. The days I left behind me seems to me a dreamland of nightmare. Our cultural continuity in social attitudes, customs, and institutions has exposed to shame by means of falsehood and

misrepresentation.' Having a wining personality, she said in a quiet and careful way. She had very little sight in her right eye.

'Why do you say so, madam?' asked the room-mate. Her words were almost a scream.

'The heart is forgetful and cannot recall yesterday. The bone suffers old age, the eyes are weak, the ears are deaf, the strength is disappearing because of weariness of heart, and the mouth is silent. All taste is gone. God is becoming evil. What old age does to men and women is evil in every respect. He who thinks half-heartedly will not believe in God, but he who really thinks has to believe in God. We now see a culture intolerant of religious differences,' said Malina Dev. They heard the church bells tolled the congregation to church. Shoppers all fagged out by the Christmas rush.

'I can't understand why you say so,' said the room-mate, looking at her where she sat among the freckled shadows

'I'm feeling better about it now,' said Malina Devi gaily and on the same note of pleased surprise that was in her smile, 'Every old person proceeds with doubtful and timorous steps. Parrots in design traditionally were associated with romance and passion. Elephants are symbols of wealth, royalty and fertility. And Old age is associated with hate and neglect. Do you know the meaning of Old People's Home?' She threw an anxious glance at the doors that opened on to the verandah.

'No. I don't know,' said the room-mate in cold voice. Her gaze went past her and she spoke to the servant who lingered by the door: 'Bring a glass of water for the madam.'

'The meaning of Old People's Home is where your heat is not fluttered with a vague terror. Your mind is not beaten to the ground by the catastrophe. The road to Old People's Home is smaller and less important road leading off a main road. Do you know why I say this?'

'I don't. Why?' said the room-mate

'Our family ---it is like the clothes we wear, which warm us, not with their heat, but with ours. We can't waste time in advance. The next year, the next day, the next hour are lying ready for everybody, as perfect, as unspoiled, as if we had never wasted or misapplied a single moment in all our life. I don't lie in unhappy imagination. The wretched life mistakes the matter. Truly speaking, I don't feel myself yesterday.'

The room-mate was clever at understanding and making judgements about the boarders of Old People's Homes. She gave a pleasant smile: the smile an actress might have employed to indicate pleasurable surprise.

'What a beautiful comment it is! May God give you good morrow! Times are hard. Old persons hardly move with the times---the timeless themes of love, solitude, joy, and nature. Do you feel better at this age?' said the room-mate with a catch in her voice. She asked Malina Devi with a lively, supple voice. Malina Devi looked out at the stars inspiring suprarational dreams against all silly-jeering idiots of society.

"Why not? Love perfumes the night and flourishes under the grave. The aged individuals today are often ostracized, neglected, and overlooked; elders are seen no longer as bearers of wisdom but as embodiment of shame. They are consistent in their negative attitude as the young harbouring negative attitudes about them. Today half of older adults suffer multi-morbidity---prolonged sickness, dependence, pain, and suffering. How long will I suffer these abominations in the soulless concrete blocks of Old People's Home?' said Malina Devi bluntly. Both remained silent and looked at each other.

'The joys of parents are secret, and so are their griefs and fears. My life isn't mine if I always care what others. All old persons accept humiliation, under duress, at an intolerable sacrifice. Every successful and unsuccessful person has one thing 'common'---'24 hours in a day'. Only difference is ....How they 'utilise' it.'

Malina Devi unloaded her bitter feelings. The lovely colour faded from the room-mate's cheeks. Looking at the uniform red brick houses, she thought all her dreams were coming true at last.

She knew that the majority of men, when faced with such a query from a woman, would resort to denial or some soothing generality. The Old People's Home was full of noise, and the rooms with their walls painted. Their windows screened with stone tracery were stiflingly cold. Below the balconies lay paved courtyard and gardens thick with mango and gold-mohur trees. The truant boys, sitting under the trees, were seen having a tasty bit of gossip. The roads petered out into a dirt track and would tax them with neglect of study in future.

'With due respect, I would like to say a simple thing cannot be divided and analysed. Sinners are around us. They make the boundary as our sons and daughters discriminate between parents and them. This discrimination is actually as infectious and as dangerous as the plague. Have you been to post-office today as before?' enquired her room-mate.

Malina Devi looked sad and nodded gravely as her room-mate poured out a trouble-shooting question. She said: 'You know my only son, after marriage, has been in America for over eight years. But I haven't got any single letter from him since he left India. The more we think of our sons, the less they do their duty for their parents. He who has no children knows not what love is. The sons are selfish today, having no feelings for their parents. I feel my sufferings unmitigated by any hope of early relief. To live longer is a curse, indeed. Once to die is better than the length of days in sorrow without end. I must unpack my heart with words. This is the consequence of my unrequited love for my son. I desire nothing today but the reward of my son—a villain and a cursing hypocrite. To live in Old People's Homes is as black as hell and as dark as night. I know the road to my death will go on for miles and miles. Gee, it's a screw life.'

Her eyes brimmed with tears. It caused a lot of bad feelings, not least among the boarders whose lives she knew. She laid about herself with her stick to keep the little sitting on the window sill.

'Why do you say so, madam' asked the room-mate, looking fixedly with wide-open eyes

Looking at her, Malina Devi twisted her body to the left, then to the right. She then spoke clearly, unlike the others: 'Old persons are national liabilities. At this age, every minute lost is a neglected by-product; once gone; you will never get it back. The body is like a piano, and happiness is like music. It is needful to have the instrument in good order. Death will seal up all in rest as after sunset day fades in the west. I see no life in this Old People's Home. At this age everything is out of order. Behind me I hear the same man asking: where is God now? I wish God be at my end, and at my departing. ' She shook as if she were crying, but she made no sound. Her years of living in Old People's Home had taught her valuable lessons of depression resulted from fatigue and poor health.

The room-mate rushed forward and put her consoling arm around her shoulders. New ideas were simmering in the back of her mind. She then gave a well-thought and consistent argument: 'our life in old age should be centered on love—love for God and love for our fellow being. If each person awakened to the oneness of all life, there would be peace and happiness in our old age. Keep away from the pretentious parade of sons' empty promises. Don't cry, madam. I think every Old People's Home is a gracious union of excellence and experience. Feeling is better that thinking. Every old person will do the same thing till the pangs of death shake him.' Malina Devi was emotionally unsound and gave a shy smile at her room-mate.

'How can I be able to expand my inner space? How can a mother stop seeing others' negative qualities? Every mother's love is translated into thoughts, words and deeds that are expressed in kindness to others---unimpeachable evidence. Every mother has an unearthly love for her sons and daughters. But they put on a false appearance of virtue and act in contradiction to their stated beliefs and feelings. Mental strength is the stem of thoughts. I had a real lust for life.' She said in low voices.

Her words made the room-mate look sick and shied away from consoling her with sympathy. Her silence signalized approval. She gave her sorrow fire

three times with sighs. The room-mate got to feel why she always felt unhappy and unrestrained.

Her room-mate nodded and leaned forward in her chair, and she clasped hands on her knees and her head silvered by the moonlight coming out from the window. She remained silent as the depth of night. At night, all streets and lanes became menacing as the city was infested with an ivy league of criminals and gamblers. They moved secretly like a lion in his den. Citizens didn't know how to separate good-looking pecans from culls.

The last months had been full of anxiety and strain and infuriating frustration for Malina Devi. Her talking to other boarders had driven her hazardously near to a breaking-point. All other boarders were of the same condition as her.

Looking at her worried-looking face, Malina Devi said: 'A few questions are always peeping into my mind. The questions are anathema to most of the elderly persons. You know, old age is solitude of atrophy, of negation, but of perpetual deflowering. In old age, every person, I think, sails through all sorts of contradictions. To express plaintively is the last phase of life. To live a despicable life of widowhood in India has always been discouraging. Most of the age-old women---having lost their husbands by death---have passed through a painful period in Old People's Home. The Hindus and the Mohammedans recoil together in horror from sacrilege and defilement....'

The room-mate interrupted the speaker with a question: 'Why do you say so?'

Malina Devi said in a cheerful and lively way: 'The real reason lies deeper. Communalists are always bound by authoritarianism, orthodoxy and traditional forms of superstitions. Panic spreads with the incredible swiftness and sweeps out across India. And our fear lends to evil tidings. Distress likes dumps when time is kept with tears. We need a statesman who exercises political leadership wisely and without narrow partisanship.' Her calm manner lulled the room-mate into a false sense of security. The moonlight was low and romance was in

the air. Although she grew up in Bengal, She had always had a taste for the vibrant lights.

She got to know the majority of age-old morning walkers of Old People's Homes were apt to find journeys all over the city uncomfortable, fatiguing and insufferably tedious, but she had an interest and enchantment in every mile of the way: in the sun-baked silence of the dusty roads and the cheerful tumult of the have-nots and slum-children. How could anyone travel through such a country and find it, as Lord Auckland's sister, Emily Eden, had found it, 'a shriveled cinder of a country', and 'quite hideous'?

'I have already attained a ripe old age. I am seized by a helpless, foolish pang of pure jealousy. What are your questions?' The room-mate asked inordinately curious about it, staring with huge luminous eyes.

The warm, moonlit stillness of the garden was another world which had nothing in common with the turmoil and tensions and restlessness that were a part of the daylight hours. She turned back to her contemplation of the stretch of gardens beyond the trees, as though her interest in what lay there had absorbed her attention to the exclusion of all else. She now made her attention to her room-mate.

'Do you know Pratima Devi, aged about 80, living in this spacious Old People's Home? Her room has been vacant for over two months. Where does she have gone?' asked the room-mate inordinately curious about the matter

Malina Devi's lower lip trembled. She had suffered a lot of problems with her lower back. After a persistent request, Malina Devi stood up and went right to the door. She closed the door softly, getting back to her seat. Dazzled by the glamour of dark and forbidding city life, she had lost her attractive and exciting quality.

'I'm feeling tired,' she said, 'three months ago; her son and daughter-in-law accompanied her mother on a ten-day tour of Rajasthan. Ten days later, her son and daughter-in-law got back home, leaving his mother alone to an unknown and solitary station. I don't know whether she is alive or not. Her life

in old age has turned into a still-born venture. She has always been stung with remorse in her room. She is extremely tired at this age.' She bent from the waist and brought her head down to her knees. She tried remembering her past days. She was of a noble blood. Over the years she had tried to block out that part of her life.

'Humans are so innately violent! By misfortune Pratima Devi gave birth to a mentally disoriented mischievous son. Prostrated with anguish, she felt weak, shocked, and unable to do anything. To get an apology from his mother is to get blood from a stone. The whole incident drove her son crazy. The problem should not be passed over lightly.' The room-mate said in a distressing heart. The story brought to tears in her eyes.

Raising her head, Malina Devi said, 'Living in this Old People's Home has me get much experience in this crying world. I have taken the wrong road by mischance. Truly speaking, I had never had such a great adversity of a woman as Pratima Devi. I have also lost even in the depths of misfortune. Those who take the greatest care still make mistakes.' She then clutched her walking stick protectively.

An indescribable sound rose from the crowd; a soft growling snarl of a street dog, and Malina Devi rose and stepped forward, and facing the quarter from whence the stone had been thrown, raised her voice and called a jest across the heads of the crowd. It was a coarse and untranslatable jest, relative to the proper treatment of prostitutes, and the crowd, taken by surprise, laughed.

'Thank you for being so forbearing,' said the room-mate,' your son doesn't know family relationships are stronger than any others. Understanding the truth of our identity, of being a Soul, changes how we perceive ourselves and the world around us. A little awareness enables us to experience soul consciousness in every scene.'

Malina Devi uttered no sound, lowering her head down.

'Yes, you're right. When we are ego-conscious, we believe our self to be a body, role, position, and a relationship and then we look for peace, happiness, love, and power in them. We radiate love and affection to our sons and daughters. If any old person doesn't get any help and encouragement from his supportive family, his condition is like a bird without wings; if he soars he falls to the ground and dies. I will ask you some elementary questions. How are we growing old? Why are we sick at this age? Why do we not act at our own discretion? Can you tell me why aged individuals today are often ostracized, neglected, and overlooked? Do you have had any answer to my questions?' said Malina Devi, giving an alluring smile.

'I think I don't have all the answers to your questions?' said the room-mate.

Malina Devi said further: 'There is a change in society. We are not, we cannot, in the nature of things, be, what our fathers were. There is nothing permanent except change. Weep not that the world changes. We should be wise and discreet, when our old age appears.' She had never ever believed she would have lived in Old People's Home—unfriendly and frightening. The air was full of fugitive strains of old song from a distance place. Tears of outraged vanity blurred her vision. She was often nostalgic recalling of experiences long past and gone. She had got much revelatory experience about family life that she had not known before. Credited with extraordinary moral and spiritual insight, she recalled the words of the poem:

'What is it to grow old?

Is it to lose the glory of the form,

The lustre of the eye?

Is it for beauty to forge her wreath?

---Yes, but not this alone.'

The room-mate got pleased at her presentation. 'Is it enough, my respected lady? A large proportion of old people live alone. All boarders will respect you as long as you play fair. The elders are seen no longer as bearers of wisdom but as embodiment of shame. The starving multitude is in want of the bare necessities of life. When the sun becomes yellow, it quickly declines,' said the room-mate with a gesture of despair.

Her voice had a sudden tremor of fear in it, and she put out a hand and caught at her sleeve: 'My respected lady, the elders need a sharp lesson of how to live up with dignity against all hazardous situations. Look all around the city. The city is blazoned with red flags. Comrades have an unquestionable loyalty to their leaders without knowledge of certain facts. Music is blazing from the loud speakers. We're now living in a frenzied society full of abnormal excitement and emotional disturbance. Honestly speaking, every ageing person, like a wounded bird, pierced with sharp arrows, is whining and pining for survival.' She clenched her fist in anger.

There was exasperation and bitterness in Malina Devi's gesture, as though some prophetic vision of the future of old persons had raised before her in all its tragic futility.

She was stern and cold in appearance and seemed to have painted an authentic picture of old age. Her deep breathing became steady. There were things moving across the open ground between the sharp-edged shadows of buildings. Things that moved in complete silence--- keeping for the most part to the shadows and flitting noiselessly across the moonlit spaces like a frieze of trolls--- bowed, hunchbacked and grotesque, silhouetted briefly against the silver-washed grass or the wall of a house; lost again in shadow and emerging only to be swallowed up by the ground.

She got used to drinking air into her lungs like all other morning walkers. On every Sunday, she drank herself into oblivion in presence of droning mosquitoes making a sustained deep murmuring, humming, and buzzing sound all over the room. She drank so as to forget her bygone days of despair and

desolation when she had spent the days in monotonous activity and in idleness. She had become depressed and weakened.

As her eyes became accustomed to the shadows, she could make out the curving line of the long lashes, the faint, puzzled crease between her eyebrows, and a stray tendril of grey hair that curled childishly above her ear. Malina Devi then said, looking at the waxing moon:

'Is it to feel our strength—

Not our bloom only, but our strength---decay?

Is it to feel each limb

Grow stiffer, every function less exact,

Each nerve move loosely strung?'

The room-mate picked her words carefully and said slowly: 'I am in agreement with your animated discussion. Half of older adults suffer multi-morbidity---prolonged sickness, dependence, pain, and suffering. In fact, so much so that I will tell you something that few people are aware of it. We are diverging from each other. We open during the day and close at night like flowers. Do you know Kalpana Devi, aged about 83, living in this Old People's Home? She is very good woman.' The room-mate looked at Malina Devi in a blank incurious stare.

'I know her. A good name is like sweet-smelling ointment. Old age and death complement each other. What happens to her?' asked Malina Devi with inquisitive mind and intense excitement, chewing pan together with a betel-nut.

The room-mate said in her sorrowful eyes, 'Whenever you come across with her, she looks miserable. Kalpana Devi, having an aureole of youth and health, was born and bought up in the upper class of society. Her only son after marriage went to America for higher education. After three years, he came back to Calcutta to take his uncaring elderly mother to America. Unfortunately, Kalpana Devi could not realize his deceptive motive. Three weeks later, her son sold out the three-storied building to a tycoon. The bulk amount of money was then ploughed back into his own bank account in America. Never did she imagine her son's hypocrisy and nasty trick with suspicion. She always stood muted before her son. Most people don't realize that they are breathing. We are fighting for our own existence at this age.'

Malina Devi said in a cold voice: 'Ouch! I know how it is. God---don't I know! Sometimes I've laid awake at night feeling like that. There are so many women whom one could follow blind. But not even a hundred good men can undo the harm that one son can create. Helping to sow the wind in the pious hope we shall reap the subsequent whirlwind.'

The room-mate gave a satiric look at the increasing complexity of Bengal society and said: 'Life in old age is worse than being dead. At this age, I feel depressing circumstances of old age, inside and outside, are looming large day by day. Animals are happy, trees are happy, birds are happy. The whole existence is happy, except man. Only man is so clever that he creates his own unhappiness---nobody else seems to be so skillful. To give birth to a child in one thing---to be a mother is totally different.'

'Wow! What happened to Kalpana Devi?' asked the room-mate

She remained silent for a moment and said: 'On the day of departure, her only son with his wife whisked off by plane for America pleasurably, leaving his elderly mother at departure lounge at Dumdum airport. She didn't know what happened to her. After an hour, she got to know her son's hypocrisy and cant. She then ploughed her way through the waiting passengers at departure lounge. Goodness knows, she now shuts herself away in her room for hours. She doesn't have any contact with anyone. Her son returned the insults with interest. What a sign of the times! Now she looks at the crescent moon, hidden behind the tamarisk tree outside my window, as if the dear departed one is smiling and playing hide-and-seek with me. Truly speaking, the cultural anthropology of India has declined gradually since independence. Finding no alternate way, she has sheltered in an angle of this building. A life of leisure eventually begins to pall. At present she takes pleasure in her troubles, keeping

apart from other boarders to a quiet life. There is a psychological instability everywhere. Her sons and daughters-in-law have devoured her resources.'

Malina Devi surveyed the scene with a sardonic smile as she spent a few quiet hours in solitude. Everything was hidden from her sight behind some trees. She knew there was a steady increase of neglected parents in all sections of Bengal. There was a stink of corruption in all sections of society and a sordid avariciousness and a morbid pleasure in hoarding. Breezes were blowing deviously.

'I don't know what you say,' said her room-mate further, 'Never have I had such a depressing experience as Kalpana Devi got at this age. We, like the homeless, live with misery every day. I think it happened as if by fate. She was obviously caught in the net of suspicious circumstances. She fought for her honour and for life. I shall try to keep her plentifully supplied with gossip and humour. She could hardly feel a sudden sharp apprehension and fear resulting from the perception of imminent danger. Can I tell you something, my respected lady?' She met her steady gaze. Malina Devi's face was broodingly morose.

'Why not?' Malina Devi said in mournful eyes, 'I do not want to hear a horrific account of the tragedy. I'm not a sour and disheartened woman. I'm living in my own little world and passing the last days of my life in this building looking gloomy and forbidding like the living people of a drowsy village. You know an old person who is abandoned by near ones is dear to remote ones. Everyone interprets us incorrectly. 'Malina Devi covered her face with her apron-strings to hide out gloomy face. She took approximately five minutes. The room-mate looked at her approvingly and nodded.

After having a relaxing mood, Malina Devi further said: 'I believe in myself; I don't believe in anything else. Do you know Nero, Emperor of Rome, murdered his mother and executed or murdered most of his relatives? Even he kicked his pregnant wife to death. Nero was not forthright in appraising his problem. Man can ordinarily have two kinds of character. One is the negative character: the character of the criminal, the character of the anti-social, the

character of the rebellious, and the character of selfishness. Her son has those qualities of negative character.' The room-mate couldn't rein her impatience.

'What is the positive character?' said the room-mate, steadily looking at Malina Devi. Her curiosity was aroused by the mysterious character of man. She sat comfortably with the rhythm of her breathing, releasing her pent-up emotions.

Malina Devi got satisfied at her curiosity. She said: 'another is the positive character: the character of the conventional, orthodox, respectable. The society is very murderous about the negative. And naturally, on the other hand, the society respects. Every woman in old age is a daughter of Hope and Fear. In old age, we become so ill that we can no longer make decisions about anything.'

Her anxiety was gnawing her to know the mysterious character of man. The room-mate said anxiously: 'Is it so? I think Nero was hardly guided by a high sense of honour and duty in childhood. I don't know what happens today. Husbands today have been stepping out on their wives. After the birth of my son, I thought my son's kindness would restore my faith in human nature. I didn't know my son laughed at and played tricks on his mother. The misery is general, where not glossed over by liberal application of alcohol. Every old person has been alienated from the selfish values of our present society and family. We fail to dispense wisdom to the students.' The room-mate said, looking at a favourite resort for the rich and famous.

The room-mate became very depressed, anxious and tired, and couldn't deal with normal life. She was getting more and more irritated at Nero's behaviour towards his mother and wife. She felt an irregular heartbeat in a strikingly clear and sparkling air. She was trying to gloss away the irrationalities of the universe.' The story withered her with a look. Her face was dark with rage.

A few moments later, she felt comfortable. Malina Devi said: 'Do you feel uncomfortable now?

'No, I don't. We are as God made us,' the room-mate said, with a forced smile

'There is a saying among our people that those whom the gods would destroy them first make mad. Life will always move in the direction. Today will never happen. Every night has been unruly to me---to say nothing, to do nothing, to know nothing, and to have nothing. For all I know I'm still living in this Old People's Home. At this age I have a very bad memory to forget things easily. Even the high-pitched sound gives out a horrid discordant noise. If there be no son to perform the funeral rites, the low-minded people believe that there can be no resurrection to eternal bliss. Age looks all ways, and ponders wisely on the past.' Malina Devi's face was suddenly scarlet with rage.

She breathed a sigh of disappointment and stared at her wide-eyed. She knew hundreds and thousands of age-old beggars, driven out by their sons, got to Calcutta. With bowed heads they supplicated their Lord.

Looking at her weather-beaten face, the room-mate said in a low voice, 'Never give up. Today is hard, tomorrow will be worse, but the day after tomorrow will be sunshine. For you to have survived such an ordeal is remarkable. How to spend the last days of my life is for me to decide. No woman is educated who is not equal to the successful management of a family. This outmoded and rigid society makes an old person fossilized. So you must really not expect us to make a public exhibition of ourselves by ordering a forsaken mother, just because you yourself feel nervous! I think a repentant sinner vows to submit to the will of God.' She repressed her anger.

Malina Devi got pleased at her fine-sounding words and said, holding her palms together: 'I pray, cease your counsel, which falls into my ears as profitless as water in a sieve. My intelligence is true; my jealousies are reasonable. Don't give me counsel.' The room-mate hadn't the remotest idea of what was going on. Remarkably, she was not hurt.

Malina Devi deliberately said to her India that had once seemed to her so glamorous and beautiful a country began to wear a different aspect. She knew

now, underneath that glamour and beauty there lurked undreamed-of depths of cruelty and terror, just as the graceful minarets and gilded domes of the palaces rose above narrow, filthy streets and the squalid hovels of the poor. At night criminals and reputed mobsters, sneaking around the Old People's Home, were having fun in a noisy way after drinking country liquor.

The room-mate threw a sidelong look at Malina Devi to see if she had noticed her blunder. She looked quickly through the papers, sifting out from the pile that looked interesting. She said dryly, 'I envy your optimism. The empty Old People's Home seems so lonesome. The crowd dispersed, melted away into the side streets. Look down, look down that lonesome road. My favourite age is 40. I haven't yet diagnosed the problems of our old age. Take a chance to dice with death.'

She made a loud sound by breathing air out with annoyance. The ceiling fan creaked and flapped gently and monotonously overhead and a pair of lizards on the wall behind the desk chirruped a small, shrill counterpoint.

'Why?' asked Malina Devi. Her curiosity was aroused by the mysterious number. Her anger melted away.

'I mean,' said the room-mate categorically, 'Age 40 makes us recognise that some doors are closed to us forever. Forty is to decide when we know that we are unlikely to live forever. At 40, all women are good at sniffing out a scandal of housewives. At 40, we don't care what others think of us. At 60, we discover they haven't been thinking of us. And the sharp awareness that the trip is half over can make us act, and react, in drastic and sometimes unexpected ways. At 40, parental love is unconditional and survives even rebuffs in return. Judicious parents always use kindness and discipline in equal measure. The boarders of this old People's Home live in a vacuum so that the world outside them is of no moment.' There was an odd note of bitterness in her voice. Malina Devi gave a vacant smile.

'You would like to say, at 40, we start understanding that we, and everyone else, are bundles of extremely mixed emotions. And eventually we

can accept that fact and live with a lot more ease inside our own skin. Life is full of triggers. Negative triggers are sorrow and suffering, and positive trigger is the joy that comes from expanding the circle of love beyond the biological family. A sensible woman is not fooled by flattery. At 40 we have the energy, the clarity and the focus to know what we want and how to get it. I take a healthy diet that can help prevent heart disease. Medicine is often recommended for the patients suffering from arthritis,' said Malina Devi confidently, looking at her reflectively.

The room-mate looked at her and thought hard for a few moments. Leaning towards her, she whispered: 'For 40, I think, is when we begin to know ourselves, to belong to ourselves, in a comfortable, honest and ---yes---forgiving way. Forty is when we grow clearer about our strengths and capabilities and more at peace with our failings and flaws. But....'

Malina Devi interrupted: 'I do agree with you. At 40, we also accept our darker feelings and wishes, our envies and angers and wicked thoughts. At 40, we start understanding that we, and everyone else, are bundles of extremely mixed emotions. And eventually we can accept that fact and live with a lot more ease inside our skin.'

Malina Devi broke into sobs. 'Will...my son will be all right?' she asked, looking at the scratch on the side of her looking glass.

'I can't be sure at this point,' said the room-mate, 'Why do you get angry at this age?'

'Rubbish!' Malina Devi murmured under her breath, 'You know anger leads to clouding of judgement, resulting in bewildering of memory. Every old person gets angry when children do not obey them. Every old person gets angry when scolded in public. Every old person gets angry when his colleague blunders. Every old person gets angry when spoken of behind his back. The list is endless.'

The room-mate got much pleased at her soothing analysis.

Malina Devi further said: 'I know it very well. I remained sane even in times of crises. Do you know time heals griefs and quarrels; for we change and are no longer the same persons? The Old People's Home is the language of grave. We want to sing here like the birds sing, not worrying about who hears or what they think. We need a hygienic view of national realities and moral imperatives. I do my work and then loaf the rest of the day.' She looked out the window with wishful eyes. She saw a van park at the side of Old People's Home. She realized they were surrounded on all sides

The room-mate got to feel that the experience had moulded and coloured her whole life. Most of the neglected old persons suffering from social deprivation had finally taken shelter in Old People's Homes in a desperate attempt to save themselves from the hands of their sons and daughters-in-law. Most of them moved with a staggering motion and clumsily from side to side as they had a condition of deep suffering from misfortune and affliction.

Something niggled at her heart. 'I don't know what to say,' said desperately unhappy Malina Devi, 'You have nothing to lose by telling the truth. In old age the old persons spend a lot of our lives wandering round with their eyes shut, bemoaning their fate. Every minute in old age lost is a neglected by-product; once gone, we will never get it back. In old age, the old parents are treated like domestic servants to look after their grandchildren. They are served with a malnutritious meal whereas we served our sons and daughters faithfully for many years. There is the remotest possibility to allay our fears. I have seen enough of the world. We live in the religion of idolatrous nationalism. It is a proven record.' The room-mate didn't give any quick and witty reply. A few minutes later, she said:

'How can we change our miserable conditions in old age?' asked the room-mate anxiously

Malina Devi let out a long deep breath to show that she was disappointed and sad. She said: 'Options have narrowed and some doors are closed, but, consider the doors you are starting to open---now that you've got the wherewithal to walk through. I have watched so many friends refuse to walk

through those doors and live into their own life in this tumultuous decade that starts at 65.'

'It's perfect!' the room-mate exclaimed. 'At 65, it makes our waist look smaller; our legs look longer and slenderize our hips.'

Looking at her, Malina Devi gravely said, 'Mahadev Basu—the gentleman is wise—often says 'In old age we can differentiate between yesterday and today and tomorrow. Can you tell me why Monday is so far away from Friday but Friday is so close to Monday? All are same to us. Who is the happy person?'

She stared hard at the room-mate. She then gathered up the heavy tresses of her hair, and confined them beneath her head.

'I am blithely unconcerned about it. Who is he?' asked her room-mate. Her grey hair dropped on her pallid cheeks.

'Do you not know him? The happy person is one who is happy even when there is unhappiness. Try to understand it. The happy person is one who understands life and accepts its polarities. Mahadev Basu is that happy person who teaches the strictly-forbidden slum children every morning, sitting around unexpected circumstances, behind the Old People's Home---an establishment providing residence and care for the elderly with special needs. He teaches according to student ability. It is a great success by any yardstick. He has inseminated an unquestioning faith in education among the slum areas. He wants liberation from ignorance and illusion and attempts to sanitise all historical accounts.'

She remained silent for a moment and took a glass of water. Illness at this age sapped her of the energy. She told again, hiding the truth about herself so as to gain an advantage over her room-mate:-

'He feels completely at home in this Old People's Home. After the death of his only son, he lost his beloved wife, Anupama Devi. When his wife died, his entire world was turned upside down. Not to live alone in a deserted-looking room all day long, he had to leave his paternal house in effable disgust and took

refuge in Old People's Home. Never does he think over the far distant future as we don't. He has still been mourning for his lost son while teaching the children like a fatherly old man. He has a belief and trust in and loyalty to God. The children look more cheerful to take lessons from him. Do you believe it?' She was suddenly filled with a warm, shinning happiness and an assurance of immortality.

She asked her from the depths of despair and observed family gatherings with detached amusement. The room-mate remained silent. She only stared at her. An hour later she took a last anxious look at herself in the looking-glass, wished yet again that she possessed Elizabeth Taylor's blue eyes and yellow curls. She heard someone enter the room behind her and close the door. Much as she admired her thoughts and manners, she had no wish to speak further.

'Who are you waiting for?' asked Malina Devi, stuffing her mouth with pan leaves

Malina Devi said in a cool, steady voice: 'Good gracious! I am expecting my friend. I will wait in the courtyard, I think. It is quite pleasantly cool out there now that the sun is so low.' She steadied her voice with an effort, doing her best to keep it light and level. She then walked quietly towards the door.

Mahadev Basu stood quite still. His dark eyes widened a little and a pulse beat at the base of his throat. His flushed face and over-bright eyes and the slight slurring of his voice were sufficient indication that he was not entirely sober. When the shimmer of golden sun was shaking through the trees, a handsomely dressed Mahadev Basu, aged about sixty eight, came to a well-furnished Old People's Home in a quiet morning of Calcutta in 1987 in a rustle and a twitter of birds and the hoarse cawing of a crow: the chatter of a squirrel and the creek of a wheel: a conch blowing in the distant temple and a muezzin crying the call to prayer from the minaret of mosque. A glad spring morning was approaching in a full of brightness and cheerfulness. Butterflies began to come to pretty flowers. It was a rare and dazzling order of beauty.

Everything around the city was an air of mystery but nature. Artificially, he was ventilated a patient in respiratory distress. He had vented himself in a fiery letter to the editor about the untold sufferings of the elderly in 1986. As he came into Old People's Home, the damp bathrooms were ground for fungi. He got a fetid swamp. It was misty, inchoate suspicions that all was not well with him. His nature disposed him to trust others as all other elderly persons did. He surveyed the scene with a sardonic smile.

Looking up at the sky, Mr. Basu muttered: 'Anyone who has flown knows that from the air our world, with its mountains, deserts, rivers and farms, takes on new and unexpected dimensions. Unfortunate is he who passes the last days of life in Old People's Home. It is no longer desirable for the sons of today to live with their parents who have become more liability than an asset to the family. His fantastic and uncompromising sons had the habit of being swelled with fury. They didn't rely on my instincts to pull me through. I will remember it to my dying day. I have entertained grave doubts about the sons since they married. Now I face earthy problems of daily life. It is a fantastic world inhabited by monsters like a disorderly courtroom can seriously tarnish a community's image of justice. Crises in old age can only illuminate how independent we all are. Old age only imbibes moral principles. Thank heavens I'm safe! I gather my desire to be alone without a word in this Old People's Home.' He then looked up at the sky and said: 'O the All-holy, Maker of all things, forgive me.'

'Thank you, Mr. Basu,' said his friend in a colourless voice and in a slumberous eyes, 'Shame on our self-seeking and time-serving sons. They inflicted extreme pain upon their old parents.' He wiped out his tears with a small square piece of cloth.

A melancholy monster beat on his heart. He viewed the situation with alarm, giving a satiric look at contemporary society of India where at first glance the people seemed harmless enough.

Looking up at the heavens, he further said in the name of God the Merciful and Compassionate, 'O angels of death come and take me. As I grow in age, I will go in frustration. I become more miserable. At this age, the eyes are

weak, the ears are deaf, the strength is disappearing because of weariness of the heart and the mouth is silent and cannot speak. Death comes close and the goal doesn't come---that's what energy is. That is what frightens me,' thought Mahadev Basu grimly, tightening his grip on the walking-stick

He felt disheartened as he heard the news of some desperately lone old persons in their own house was frequently murdered at the hands of a few miscreants. Citizens didn't respect their elders as a valuable resource.

As he heard the news, Mr. Basu said to his fellow morning walkers: 'When I get to know it I have no sleep at night. Ever and again I open my door and look out on the darkness, my friends! I can see nothing before me in my airy room; I wonder where my path lies! My life stretches before me alluring and various as the open road. After the death of my wife and son, I think yesterday is but today's memory and tomorrow is today's dream. Always Judge people by their actions. To meet, to know, to come and then to part is the sad tale of many a heart. Heaven and hell are states of mind. When we get angry with others in old age, we lose our balance; our blood pressure rises and limbs tremble.'

He suddenly became very tearful, shedding tears of pain and heart-felt agony. Two of his fellow morning walkers came close to him putting consoling arms around his shoulders.

As he turned off his head, he saw a piece of wooden board hung on the hook. It had some information on it. It was displayed inside the Old People's Home. With a great resourcefulness of thought, he walked up close to the board and read it with a rapt attention:

'Blessed is the man that walks not in the counsel of the wicked, nor stands in the way of sinners, nor sits in the seat of the scornful. Life is uncharted territory. The seen is deeper hidden than the unseen.' A new trouble was dawning on his thickening mental vision.

Reading the message, he felt lonely and forsaken and spoke to himself: 'If it be a sin to covet honour, I am the most offending soul alive. Beauty is not something imposed but something immanent. In this boundless universe, I am

too busy with immediate concerns to worry about the future. In old age our life is as slippery and smooth as a serpent.'

He took off his shoe and removed the offending pebble. As he left the place in the calm of his solitary life, he saw a forlorn lost child going naked down in a leisurely walk. He spoke to himself: 'The country has not amended the situation since independence. The communist movement in Bengal has taken a fiendish pleasure in hurting people and restrained civilized people filled with rage, lust and violent passion. To produce a future generation that is weaker than ours is a terrible crime against humanity. The social infrastructure is imploded from greed and factionalism. Our real gift to the next generation is not business, money, gold. It is soil.'

He stood there for a few minutes. His hair was streaming back in cold. He paced back very carefully and slowly, weeping partly through sorrow, and partly through anger. He flexed his numbed fingers and smiled wryly into the darkness. How many times during the last four or five years had he longed for the sight of grey skies and the smell and the bite of east winds blowing across Bengal soil? His hands, encased in heavy gauntlets, were so frozen that he could barely feel the walking stick and his feet ached with cold. The older waiting-woman mopped the tears from her wrinkled face and chuckled like a parrot.

The older serving woman of Old People's Home, a stout grey-haired old lady, threw up arms with a little wailing cry: 'Aie! Aie! You left me alone for ever. Your words died on my lips, but you remain alive.' All at once there were tears in her eyes and her voice was a shaken whisper. 'Come and sit on my lap again, my son. I'm here in this Old People's Home.' She was crying in a loud high voice.

The brightening light beat against his closed eyelids and the grey fog in his brain lifted and shredded away like mist drifting off the river in the early morning, and slowly and almost imperceptibly the pain in the heart lessened and peace took its place. He suddenly felt old and weary. He wanted to escape from the shadows of his selfish friends and didn't want to cast another shadow on their happiness. The disagreement over property had soured relations

between fathers and their sons. He had had a lot of unpleasant events that were not likely to happen to others twice.

But this time it was real. This was the Old People's Home, standing in the leafy shade of banyan trees. The atmosphere at the house soured. A spacious balcony was for the use of boarders only. The big trees around the Old People's Home were particularly useful for brightening up shady areas. He got to feel this house wouldn't make his life happier and more enjoyable. He received a sum of money after he had been forced to retire on medical grounds. Looking at the house, he felt most of the elderly persons like him had suffered torture in their own family and had finally taken to lead sheltered lives in Old People's Homes. He knew human beings need food, clothing and shelter.

He stood quiet still, not stirring; barely breathing. He saw a figure standing in the shadows of the verandah. He was a manager of this Old People's Home. The manager, having a set of false teeth, came forward and greeted him well. His hair was short and severe. Some of his old friends had already settled there. The manager said: 'Mr. Basu—it is Mr. Basu! Why are you so late, sir? I'm waiting for you. Do you have felt any trouble on the way?'

He couldn't reply. The old, long-forgotten name from his married life returned to him. Looking up at the Old People's Home in the clouds of vaporous air all around the city, he mumbled, 'My wife died last year---I wish I could bring her back to this house towards the end of her life. I have lost two lives, so I've only got one left. Thenceforward I was forced to abrogate my responsibilities to the family. And all of my opinions were thrust aside. Sons today are always concentrating on their own advantage, pleasure and well-being without regard for others. I was crying for justice. How can I ever express my gratitude to my sons for all they have done?' He remained silent for a few moments.

He further said: 'Thank goodness for that! Unsolved problems in old age can rob me of commitment to my work and reduce me to apathy during my precious free time after retirement. How a person masters his fate is more important than what his fate is. It would make life difficult for me to start a new life here. New truth is always a go-between, a smoother-over of transitions.'

Raising his head, he looked steadily at the spectacularly impressive old traditional building. He then spoke to himself in soulful eyes: 'Much of our life is spent waiting. More is not done than I expected. So much of my life is spent preparing for distant tomorrows. Slowly I learn bits of what there is to see, and then forget and learn again. I have got no friends to speak of my agony. It is my sheltered accommodation where I can live fairly independent lives, but with staff available to help him. How will I spend the rest of my life here? Why not? I would rather live up with dignity here than live down with dishonor under my sons.' He then sang in a lively, supple voice:

'Grief wears out life, but how can we

Escape, the heart being what it is?

Had not love brought us sorrow we would be

Plagued with the sorrows of this world'

He was half dead with fear of old age as he was. His confidence was gone. He couldn't remember anything. His brain's like a sieve. Everything fell right through it. Tears were in his eyes as he thought. Three times with sighs he gave his sorrow fire. His usual quiet was almost inhuman courtesy.

He cried out without words because he was hurt and afraid. Memories came crowding in. As he cried out, other boarders were crowded behind him. They patted him back to calm down. He said: 'I'm sorry.' He wiped out his tears with handkerchief. They gave him an innocent gaze.

'Why are you crying?' said his friend, staring at him

'Smiles and tears, like sunshine and rain, are necessary for the development of life,' said he, steadily looking at him, 'Every incident has changed my life today. I feel very grateful and lucky for living in Old People's Home.'

He was safe at last. He came to a right address. The Old People's Home is spreading to the fragmented society. For him the Old People's Home was an escape from the boredom of everyday life. With a steady gaze, he looked at a steady stream of abandoned children playing on the pavement. The situation was getting steadily worse and worse under the communist rule. He was afraid of looking foolish in front of little children. He fumbled helplessly for words. 'Disgraceful!' he puffed indignantly, 'Man's a menace! A rumour-monger! They are not fit to command the loyal comrades.'

'Why'

'The young generation today defies the old periods of efflorescence of intellectual and artistic values, showing shameless boldness,' said Mr. Basu effortlessly

He then spoke in a quiet voice: 'Communists have no present, no future. Their language seems complicated but is actually without real meaning. The murky world of dirty arms will deal with them. Saying good-bye is part of every transition. The important thing is to give you time.' He paused for a moment.

A few minutes later, Mr. Basu said, 'I should have come earlier. I don't know why the police set up roadblocks on routes. People say a gang of boys was setting off fireworks on the streets. The police arrested them. The court is becoming more severe on young offenders. A prison sentence should match the severity of the crime. Many people love democracy but do not know how to defend it. Nothing is so easy as to deceive one's self.' He then stepped into his room, taking a few deep breaths to steady his nerves. As the boarders got older, they got set in their ways.

Three-weeks had already gone. He came close to others. One day Mr. Basu, with other age-old men and women, got to the river Ganges to bathe in, regardless of age. They were all co-boarders of Old People's Home. Their sons no longer had shown proper regard for their parents. There seemed to be about twenty or twenty-five persons squatting on the stone floor between the pillars. He moved forward, a step a time. He was conscious of a cold tingling sensation between his shoulder-blades and was aware that his mouth was dry. He felt that age made him physically and mentally tired. Half way through the chapter of his life he realized he hadn't taken anything from it. Very annoying was his refusal to discuss his bygone days.

He had evidently bathed in the river, Ganges, for he was clean again in the morning. The dirt and grime and powder were no longer on his face, and his hands and arms were free of morning sickness. His hair was grey and smooth from the water and he had washed out his shirt and underwear and put them on again. The saturated material clung to him wetly, moulding his slim hard body, but it was already beginning to dry in the dry heat. He saw a criminal take the revolver and the bundle of clothing from a girl.

They suddenly disappeared behind the dark entrance of a large building. There were things that he had to think about. Things must be thought about soon. But all at once he knew that he could not do it now.

A popular misconception is that the elderly persons are hazards to the society and treated like a second citizen of India. Having suffered remarkably ill-effect in old age in family life, they had to have a shelter in Old People's Homes to pass the rest of their life. They were sometimes misleadingly referred to as 'persona non grata.'

The dignity and simplicity of Maidan is full of historical curiosities. The surroundings of maidan were laced with very high and impressive buildings, deserving praise because of their high quality. Long had Maidan groaned beneath the mailed heel of the British rule and trembled at the shadow of English rulers. The British had been in India for over two centuries. Long has the ancient worship of its Gods been desecrated, and the people crushed with oppression. Men, women and children, in a word, the whole population of India had turned out to welcome the new India.

On this point, Calcutta has always suffered a lot of social, political, and educational dilemma since the dawn of independence. The older men, living all alone, were careful to be neither too soft nor too loud in their talking. So they walked up and down the maidan, swearing allegiance to the young generation.

For years the elderly persons have been ignored and not deserved to receive more attention.

Under the family circumstances, they had been a mere nonentity with no human feelings at all. And they lived totally different kinds of lives in Old People's Homes that appeared to them like the sun-god at his rising early in the morning. Cooled air was circulated throughout the old buildings, inclusive Old People's Homes. There were more anonymous faces in the crowd of morning walkers. At that time cold breeze whispered through the trees.

They couldn't get those agonizing days out of their head. The alarming rise of mental agony they had had in their own family life. For them to stay in their own house was very much difficult. They tried to drive out the thought that never entered their heads. Their sons had hazarded their lives as well as their own life and been putting such weird ideas into their heads. Trying to reason with them was like banging their heads against a wall. They hung their heads in shame, and always had their heads in religious books in Old People's Homes. Their personal unrest, alienation, and uncertainty had come from a lack of purpose.

The boarders of Old People's Homes—Mrs. Aparana Devi, Mrs. Kalpana Das, Mr. Sadashib Burman, Mr. Shibnath Mitra and others---stood head and shoulders above others advanced in years. They were suffering a crisis of confidence as all other elderly persons. Their sons and daughters-in-law had forced their parents to stop arguing over properties and behave in an insensible way. It made them feel proud of themselves in a way that their parents found annoying. Irrelevant remarks of their sons had carried them far afield. The rift between the sons and the parents had never really healed. Their destination then headed for 'Old People's Home' at last. Most of the boarders kept themselves in an irrational fear. It attacked the physical roots and symptoms of their anxiety. They didn't have mercy on their sons.

The Old People's Homes were almost close to each other and very near to maidan. Each room of Old People's Homes had only eight or ten feet square. The weed killer was applied to the lawn neat. Most of the boarders had been

forced to leave their homelands after the partition of India in 1947. They were all religious refugees. They had nothing further to say in this regard. The age-old persons got used to navigating their way to maidan through the way too narrow and shallow. They got to feel that sum of human happiness was not easy in life.

A few grey-haired naturalized Indians, born in Bangladesh, were also living in Old People's Homes. The elderly persons raised their eyebrows with an affection of surprise, looking at the eve-teasers roaming about the Dharmatala Street to take a snap of some girls standing off an unattractive building, ugly even. But there were a lot of mistakes. They were call girls waiting for their parties.

Most of the boarders had been there more than ten years. As any Hindu festival or Christmas neared, all age-old boarders became more and more excited. They must have slept five to six hours at least. Much as they were on the brink of death, the keenly alert boarders were always lively in bright smiling faces, and they managed to bring all boarders round. A few boarders celebrated the annual recurrence of a date marking a notable event, singing a devotional song.

Having celebrated the 74th birth anniversary of his wife last night with other boarders, an age-old man--barely eighty-one-- got to maidan early in the morning. He stumbled in articulation while speaking and sheltered in an angle of another Old People's Home with triplex windows. He had lost his wife, Kumudini Devi, twenty-years ago. He was listening to the long deep sound of unhappiness of the wind in the trees behind the large building. The sound was full of the usual moans and groans. He walked very carefully as he had a bypass heart surgery. He was a regular visitor to maidan where the criminals and call girls at night had been winkled out of their hiding place. As the crowd and the vehicles had thinned out, they got about the maidan in a violent, uncontrolled way.

Given that, he then said to his friend in a parched whisper: 'Do you know the death of the wife is more devastating than the death of the husband? Stuff and nonsense! I shall die and the worms will eat me,' he grunted, 'A ray of light

changes direction when it goes through at an angle. In old age we begin to trust in our natural intelligence, in our naturally wise heart, in our capacity to open to whatever arises. In old age we develop the capacity to stop hiding, to stop running away from our experience. The elderly persons always lie in between words and silences.' Saying so, he gave a little snort of laughter, wallowing in self-pity. His friend remained silent and looked at him with a regular feature.

A few moments later, the old man said in a vacuous look at the vast maidan: 'I know this maidan---there's a ruin---use it for entertainment. I get to maidan to keep healthy by eating well and to have a healthy appetite. Twice a week I eat an apple for lunch. Do you have read today's newspaper?' He moved rather gracefully with his friend

'Yes, I have,' said his friend grimly without hesitation,' There is a heart-breaking news of an elderly couple living in North Calcutta. A domestic servant was employed to take care of their clothes and served their meals etc. Unfortunately, they were brutally murdered by their domestic servant who was running away with valuable jewellery worth about two lakh of rupees. Our society distributes itself into Barbarians, Philistines and Populace. The police….' He interrupted and said, 'Stop now.'

'Why?' his friend asked on reflection, staring at him vacantly.

'Uh…what I wanted to talk to you about …uh. It is everyday's news. Calcutta is not a safe place for the elderly persons. Everything we do or say is reflective of our personality,' said he, having the eyes wide open

'What do you mean by safe place?' said his friend, 'What day is it today?'

'Today is Saturday. In a safe place there are rules. The rules are few and fair and are made by the people who live and work there, including the children,' said the old man, looking at his face.

His voice had a sudden tremor of fear in it. There was wild and ghastly scenery all around him, and a home and comfort nowhere. Indeed, the same dark scenery often rose to his mind, with reference to the whole race of age-old

persons. As concerned his own individual existence, he had long ago decided in the negative.

'We don't believe a vaguely worded statement of the police personnel. Our society is like a dead soldier. This society enjoys the process of grotesque self-deception. Can you tell me there is any safe haven for us?' asked he, looking much worried. His voice trailed off. He only showed the feelings of dizziness and fear, and of losing his balance, that was caused in some people when they looked down from a very high place. The domestic violence had left him on the verge of having a nervous breakdown.

'Thanks very much. It seems to be Old People's Home where you'll live up with dignity and with the utmost care. The Old People's Homes will produce the greatest happiness of the greatest number of anguished older people like the inexpressible grief of the bereaved parents. They have locked themselves away from the curious world. You're capable of developing and surviving independently. Let yourself off the hook. Then clear away thoughts of doom and reject the treadmill of fear as all other elderly persons do. There's no viable alternative,' said his friend, upholding his upbeat speech.

'Good God, yes! I do agree with you,' he nodded, 'during my anxiety I feel dizziness, shortness of breath, chest pain, and confusion. These sensations are frightening. Living in Old People's Home at this age is like helping to sow the wind in the pious hope that I shall reap the subsequent whirlwind. Our speech in old age, to our sons, is like a dried flower. The colour is faded and the perfume gone. And their speech is as speedy as steamroller. Most of the shadows of this life are caused by our standing in our own sunshine.' He relapsed into silence, staring meditatively at the distant walls of Governor's House.

He found himself behind a somewhat formal and symmetrical group of figures with their backs toward him, but all stiffened into attitudes as motionless as his own, and all gazing with a monotonous intensity in the direction of a handsome building. Some of the figures were in uniform. With a long breath of relief, he hurried from the maidan with his friend.

And the words were said in rich, sonorous words: 'To love, honour, and obey until death do you part.' And then he took out a passport size photocopy of his wife and kissed her for the first time. He thought she was the loveliest bride the world had ever known, and there were few who could have him wrong. The white lace looked whiter than ever against the black hair and the colour in her cheeks was more vivid than the orange blossoms in her arms, and her eyes had a happiness that surpassed understanding. As he was thinking so, the air swirled into his lungs, heavy with the scent of jasmine flowers. The old man stood enraptured, trembling inwardly at the grandeur of it.

He took a deep breath, ducked his head under and then flung himself forward with his friend, arms flailing wildly. The wife's death left him panting for breath.

The old man was tall, thin to emaciation, and his grey hair and straggling beard were already turning white. His haggard, hollow-cheeked face was scored with the lines of weariness and anxiety and the unending strain of sorrow for his colleague, who had died two weeks ago. They looked at each for a long moment and it was as if each of them had asked the other a question, and answered it. He threw out a hand in a gesture that seemed to embrace the vast maidan. There was a sudden glow in his eyes. Then he said bitterly, having a keen and farsighted penetration of judgement:

'There are so many men whom one could follow blind. But not even a hundred good men can undo the harm that my old friends can create---or a few hide-bound octogenarian, for that matter! I am not sure which is worse; the frankly venal---of whom there are mercifully few---or the aged, osseous ineptitudes which these fatuous persons force on us. My star is sinking. It makes life too complicated. '

His friend listened without interruption and shrugged his shoulders. He made a wry grimace and said: 'I am aware of it. I wish I had your singleness of purpose. Every woman searches her lover's house for his love. Today the young generation can't perceive the insight and outsight of the age-old persons

outshining most of the other persons. It's a long outstanding problem of our society and its outlying areas. What is your star, my respectable man?'

'I would like to be able to make inattentive men follow their old teachers, to damnation if necessary. There are human beings who have intelligence but who do not have the moral courage to act on it. I think moral courage without intelligence is dangerous,' said the old man promptly, 'I don't expect so.'

'Why?' said his friend

'We are all contemporaries. There is only a difference in memories, that's all. Years may wrinkle my skin, but to give up enthusiasm wrinkles the soul. Worry, fear, self-distrust bows the heart and turns the spirit back to dust. The language of teenagers today is often completely accessible to the old. The city is full of rumours. There is hope I may die young at 80. 0 wicked, wicked world--' said the old man, having a round face. He didn't express himself clearly because of emotion. His friend gave an incredulous look at the old man.

A few moments later, the old man said, 'Can I ask you a question, my friend?'

'Why not?' said his friend. He stumped off, muttering vaguely under his breath.

'Who generally takes the dead bodies of the boarders of the Old People's Home to the burial ground?' asked the old man with a sardonic smile. There was exasperation and bitterness in his voice, as though some prophetic vision of the future had risen before in all its tragic futility. His satiric look at contemporary society made him frightened.

His friend knew the Old People's Home was a large, three-storeyed building whose deep verandahs and pillared porticos looked over the beautiful, old city. It stood on high ground, among green lawns full of roses and flowering trees. It had an area of crowding, crowded buildings which housed a numberless horde of unemployed youth, entertainers, and other humble hangers-on.

'I shall give the answer as it is given to me,' said his friend, mopping his brow with a handkerchief. His question impressed him much.

Lowering his head down in shame, his friend said in gloomy and unwholesome feelings: 'Well, heaven forgive me, and all of us, I pray! Most of the boarders are generally taken to the burial ground by the local poverty-stricken slum-dwellers and local criminals who habitually are active late at night and object of producing a feeling of anxiety and terror to the city dwellers. But they are committed to the highest ethical principles that our sons haven't earned. In old age, we dealt our family problems playfully rather than seriously.'

'What a community spirit around the Old People's Home! It is as good as outright victory in old age. Truly speaking, I bask in the reflected glory of our community spirit,' said the old man in a nimble mind, 'what a moral obligation to us! But we never wished to be righteous before God and the world.' He was silent for a moment or two, stroking his beard.

When the wind was coming from behind, the old man watched that some morning walkers got to maidan, wearing shabby old jeans and T-shirts, with their worn-out cars to feel fresh air, trying to ward off a cold. They had achieved celebrity status overnight. The cars made them a status and a high income, offering to the morning walkers as particularly attractive popular features. They felt that the political leaders and bureaucrats had bargained away their freedom. Street-hawkers, uttering a harsh guttural sound, were selling out the smuggling goods down the pavements. The sellers were spirited away as the police got near them.

The morning walkers moved briskly and nimbly and then worshipped the morning sun, seeking refuge in the afternoon. They felt confused as a group of comrades, chanting and carrying placards and festoons, were shouting the same words in a rhythmic monotonous utterance with questionable trickiness. Morning walkers felt confused as they watched a distempered and disillusioned leader, having no subtlety and sharpness of discrimination, was arousing public feeling and stirring up public discussion. Some elderly persons changed the way they were walking so that they didn't walk in the same rhythm as other morning

walkers were marching with. The old man was out of step with his friend. Looking at some comrades, the old man leaned over and whispered something in his friend's ear: 'Comrades have no spiritual values in present world. China is their spiritual home more than in their own country because they share the ideas and attitudes of China. Comrades are no better than the rest of all elderly persons. It's an accurate reflection of comrades today. Their existence in this society is big, no, it's gigantic. Do you know them standing off the leader?' he asked sourly

'No. I don't know,' his friend's voice dropped to a whisper in a sullen and gloomy disposition, 'I'm concerned only with surface aspects and obvious features.'

'I know them well,' said the old man in a soft, quiet sound, 'most of them are well-advertised rapists, snatchers, and hired killers. They are clever indeed in books, but fools in practice. The leaders allow their followers to wallow in their ignorance and stifle creativity. Let's leave the place.'

'Why?' said his friend with the sublime confidence. His doubts in his mind suddenly resurfaced.

'Oh yes, very much so. Calcutta is a commonplace of unadventurous persons who seek escape reality from daydreaming. High levels of anxiety make me worried. They are unable to convey complex feelings such as gratitude, happiness, love, sadness, sympathy, embarrassment, pride, and surprise to anybody else,' said he, smoothly trimming out his hair.

The meeting came to an end on a sour note with several comrades spilling out. He heard the sound of comrades' footsteps behind them. All of his doubts had been submerged.

His hair looked as if it had been combed with his fingers. After the death of his wife, he behaved as though it was nothing to be ashamed of. And he treated any other elderly woman as though she was his own wife. His white dress and his frilly umbrella made his look as though he had come to a garden.

'Stop feeling sorry for yourself. Why do you feel so anxious?' interrupted his friend bluntly. He longed to find somebody who would understand his problems, and in him his friend had found such a person.

A gold ring glittered on his ring finger as the old man stood there with a hiccough, and he said hastily: 'Anxiety does not spare the 'haves' in old age, and rightly so. There are many questions we cannot answer, but must we not at least ask them a question? They spare no effort to make them happy. People do not live nowadays---they get about ten percent out of life. In old age, our life is a daring adventure. Rightly or wrongly, we all older persons are generally afraid of violence in the streets.' There were speeches and expressions of anguish---genuine enough at the moment of their talking. The habitual solitude of his locality was now strangely invaded by drifting sheds, agricultural implements, and fence rails from unknown and remote neighbours, and he could faintly hear the far-off calling of some unhappy workers adrift upon a spar of his wrecked and shattered Old People's Home.

He, tapping the side of his nose in an uncharacteristically curve gesture, looked back at him. He smiled in sunken cheeks and said, 'Will you stay behind after the others have gone? How much farther is our Old People's Home? I wish not to live any longer in this crying world. My only task in the morning is to sit behind the window and to look out the window to watch the office-goers and the passers-by always busy without any work. At this age, my life is obtrusively and often painfully obvious. I don't hanker after, like other old persons, money, women, and fame. I have nothing but the sky above me and the wide maidan around me. As long as I have my health, nothing else matters, my friend.'

'Why?' his friend said, looking at his worried-looking face

Two young boys went past them, making the sound of an engine running slowly, without worrying about the possible results. Conflicting emotions churned inside them. They felt emotionally confused. As the sun went down, the eve-teasers, with a heady mixture of desire and fear, would stir up the maidan into a sea of mud.

As the two young boys disappeared, singing a song with a lively, supple voice, the old man said to his friend: 'They have shamed their families. The city is a shambles after the Naxalite movement. Youth is not a time of life; it is a state of mind; it is not a matter of rosy cheeks, red lips and supple knees; it is a matter of the will, a quality of the imagination, a vigour of the emotions; it is the freshness of the deep spring of life. They do not know what they do now. However, you don't stop laughing when you grow old; you grow old when you stop laughing. Do you agree what I say?'

'Mmm, I'm not so sure that's a good idea. Nobody grows old merely by a number of years. We grow old by deserting our ideals. The effect of ever active health manifests Heaven's dreadful judgement by the visible presence of the older persons,' said his friend in a mocking smile. His answer was crisp, and he gave no details. He was tickled to discover that he had done the same thing.

'At this age,' said the old man in a grave voice,' I proceed alone into the waste, like a bold vessel leaving its haven to enter on the trackless field of the ocean. I haven't met anyone I know personally since I came into this Old People's Home. The old chair is always thrown away. I'm that old chair. I helped some of my elderly friends from their domestic violence to have a normal, useful life again after they have been very sick at heart in family life for a long time. Is it my fault? What do you say?'

He reminded him something he had done in the past. His heart was thumping with excitement as he said so. He was very upset at what to him was an offhand remark.

'I can't understand what you say,' said his friend shining his teeth white. He tried to beat a stray dog going past him. 'Don't beat an innocent animal,' said the old man, 'Don't do so.' The irritation in his voice gave his friend a sudden qualm.

'Why?' said his friend, fastening with a snap look

'The animals are at ease, relaxed; man is a tension. Look into the eyes of a cow---how peaceful, calm, tranquil she is. There is no anxiety, no anguish, and no clouds. Look into the eyes of a man!' A cold voice spoke softly into silence.

The old man said in a mischievous gleam in his eyes, 'Whenever I happen to meet my old friends, I try to penetrate to the inmost depths of my sorrowful heart. All are rubbish, to be honest. We are all, broadly speaking, middle class. And we are mostly Socialists vote-wise.'

He had been walking for two hours, and his course through the depressing monotony of the long level landscape of maidan affected him more like a dull dyspeptic dream than a dreary period of old age, performed under that sincerest of natural phenomena---Calcutta sky.

'Let me not give the answer of my question,' said his friend. The bright colour flamed up into his face.

The old man laughed again. Looking at his friend, he smiled and answered back his question: ' The old age resembles a book; infancy and old age are the blank pages, youth the preface, and man the body or most important part of life's volume. A generation of man lavishly endowed with genius. The life of everyman is a diary in which he means to write one story, and writes another; and his humblest hours is when he compares the volume as it is with what he vowed to make it. Our existential predicament is our indolence and laziness.' A great pang gripped his heart. He let out a long deep breath, feeling disappointed, sad, and tired of age.

'Yes, you're right,' said his friend smoothly running out his finger over the grizzled beard, 'Life is becoming more and more difficult at this age. The poor are oppressed by the rich, and no provision is made for the old and infirm. Do you know the meaning of old age, my friend?'

He looked blank and said he had no idea what he was asking. He only stared blankly into space.

'Tell me the meaning of old age,' said his friend, raising his eyes at the crystalline sky. And then a dry leaf crunched behind the window and Malina Devi turned quickly to see Governor's House standing in the moonlight beyond the rim of the tree shadows.

'Listen to me what I say now. Old age brings along with its ugliness the comfort that you will soon be out of it, ---which ought to be a substantial relief to such discontent pendulums as we are. In old age, one shouldn't depend on anybody, there should be no guide, there should be no teacher, and there should be no authority. There should be only oneself. People are miserable. Millions and millions of people are miserable—their misery collects like clouds. It becomes a great cloud---that is what war is. Then one day we are all surrounded in darkness, in murder, in killing each other, in rape. The little things make me slightly more intolerable.' He thanked him for the appreciative tone and remained silent

'You should be careful enough. I think music may be much the most respectable of your tastes at this age. I know old age is the most frightening time of our life. Do you feel offended at my words?' said his friend, looking at him.

A few moments later, he said, 'Not at all. Now tell me how much farther our Old People's Home is? Never had I expected that I would have lived in Old People's Home—a house of ghastly loneliness. In old age, people generally suffer from 'osteoarthritis' 'osteoporosis' heart disease, hypertension, and constipation. So it's my destiny, indeed.'

'Why?' said his friend, opening his mouth wide open.

He caught sight of an old man bent down in age. Looking at him, he said in a low voice: 'A secret enemy--a conspiracy of silence--has been continually by our side. It comes secretly as a lion. It casts a cold eye on life, on death. After long years, we sight the land of peace heaven.'

His cheeks were furrowed and written like rain-washed rags. The streets were silent and deserted.

'Hmm? Oh—mile. Get there soon. It'll take only forty-five-minutes to get there. Try not to worry. I willn't stay here for a moment and will keep an eye on the maidan. We have to set off at a steady pace.'

Looking out the window of the Old People's Home, he saw the slum-dwellers were unkempt and scruffily dressed. Their enthusiasm was infectious, but they were not inspired with a foolish and an extravagant love for communist slogans as all other unschooled comrades were infatuated. They struggled hard to free themselves from the shackles of communist party. He moved his shoulders uneasily and dragged himself to his feet. He felt uncomfortable. He bent down to shake a pebble out of his shoe. On the way out of the maidan he paused by the newspaper stall to buy a paper. What he got was the Statesman of the previous day.

'Damnation!' he exclaimed in annoyance and disgust. He shaded his eyes against the street lights. His face was in deep shadow.

'What's wrong?' asked his friend, astounded by such an outburst from him normally self-contained old person.

His friend's hand tightened on his arm. His great dark eyes were fixed on him, liquid with tears of foreboding. He said: 'Damn me, I should have been more careful of my sons.'

He couldn't be sure what the government would decide to do for the oppressed and suppressed old persons driven out by their sons. He could only wait and see.

He took the morning walk into the maidan every day to get the newspapers. And as the month went on, the importance of events in Calcutta began to fade like a flower in front of a furnace. Greater, more tragic events were taking shape.

As they walked down a tree arched over the road, they suddenly listened to the sounds of movement fade and die; all at once the maidan was intolerably still. Nothing seemed to stir in that cold, breathless stillness; no twig or leaf or dry spear of grass. The old man drew the attention of his friend as he saw a group of truant boys ten-twelve years put something into a hollow hole of a tree.

'What's up?' said his friend. He had nagging doubts about their relationship. There seemed to be nothing alive in it except themselves. He was unduly harsh and hostile in making an inquiry.

Giving an inscrutable smile, he said, 'They are all petty snatchers, contemptible persons, snatching money bags from the bus or train passengers or passers-by in presence of in-service police officers in our unsettled political conditions. They are habitually active from sunrise to sunset—a distressing scene. They create a feeling of anxiety and terror among the passengers;' said the old man, 'that hollow hole of the tree, they deposit their hundreds and thousands of rupees, is their private bank. A young snatcher sitting under the tree protects the bank account as a security guard, living in an untouched wilderness. They become a world unto themselves. '

'It's very interesting. It is like a frightening dream that awakens the sleeper,' said his friend, looking at the security guard of the private bank.

The old man suddenly noticed an age-old woman in tattered clothes, relying on a walking-stick, was stepping in to get help from a local hotel. She seemed to have been starved of food. The old man said to his friend, 'Who is that woman staying outside the hotel?'

'I know her very well,' said his friend in a good-looking face

'What happened to her? Woman, transgress not beyond the limits of Heaven's mercy!' cried the old man

His friend said soberly, 'Six months ago that old woman, driven out by her only son and daughter-in-law due to regular domestic violence, took shelter in a lonely pavement of a deserted lane of Calcutta. Next day morning a bank employee found her lying on a dusty-ridden pavement. She was crying for food.

Her eyes rested on the food for the customers. Heaven's light be her guide.' His expression was watchful and alert.

'Quite enough, everything in my life is getting disappeared into the distance,' said the old man laconically. He cleared his throat in nervous and shot a quick look at his friend that needed no interpretation.

A soft, monotonous ticking crept into the silence and he looked down and saw that it was his friend's watch which must have fallen from his pocket. He reached out and picked it up and the broken chain clinked as he lifted it. They had reached their destination---Old People's Home---by the evening. They had been dinning out that evening. They had eaten a tolerable meal in the main room of a restaurant, while the moon rose over the plain and someone played a tinkling tune on a stringed instrument.

It was a haunting thread of sound, oddly familiar, and the old man and his friend found themselves listening to it with a feeling that they had heard that particular tune before. He was very tired and anxious to get to his own room of Old People's Home. As he stepped out on to the verandah, he saw a young boy hold a girl's hand in a hard grasp with fingers that were feverishly hot and unsteady, and lifting it to his lips, he kissed it. It was not a light gesture of gallantry, but a kiss as greedily passionate as those which the old man had forced on his wife. Once he had tried to drag his hand away but his wife held it hard, kissing it again and again; moving her hot, hungry mouth against its cool softness.

The night was cold and very still. The tireless wind---the clean wind of night---sang on, fraught with ringing, rocking souls. Stars blazed like wedding ring s in the darkness and, falling on his wife, were entangled in her hair and extinguished in her tousled hair.

So still that every small sound of all the small sounds that got to make up silence separated itself from its fellows, and emphasized that stillness. The cheep of a muskrat; the dry scrape of a scorpion crawling up the wall; the flitter of a bat's wings in the dark verandah of Old People's Home; the drone of the

mosquitoes and, from very far away, the echo of a dog barking on the plains beyond the maidan. The elderly persons cast down this accursed city as their fathers had done. There has been a lack of upright citizens in Calcutta since independence. Calcutta was but a splendid gate of ruin.

Two rough-and-ready beds, a roll of matting, some tin boxes, an oil lamp and an earthenware containing water would not have been considered 'everything'---or even 'anything'---a few hours ago. The water in the earthenware was warm and stale, and there was not a great deal of it. There was a tin mug as all other Old People's Home had. They drank thirstily but sparing themselves, and wetted their handkerchiefs in it to cool their hot bodies.

Sarala Devi got to know: 'There has been a rampant growth of rambling Old People's Homes in several areas of West Bengal. Many elderly persons are admitted to an asylum due to family violence. Alas! They are undone! Such is frequently the fate when the woman has encountered, and lived through, an experience of peculiar severity. If she be all tenderness, she will die. If she survives, the tenderness will either be crushed out of her, or---and the outward semblance is the same---crushed so deeply into her heart that it can never show itself more. A variety of different sections of people---widows, widowers, forsaken husbands and other age-old persons of forthright views with untoward side effects---got to live in the wilderness of Old People's Homes. They concealed themselves behind the doors. There was an atmosphere thick with flattery and toadyism all around the crowded city of Calcutta.'

It was learnt that some Old People's Homes had formerly been hotels under the British rule. Those Homes were more prone to fracture. They looked dark and unwelcoming.

Sarala Devi, aged about 83, remained widowhood all her life, was living in Old People's Home. She was well known to all boarders of Old People's Homes. The condition of her Ill health prevented the blood from circulating freely. It concerned her well, and she was anxious for her safety as all other boarders suffered. She got into the room with much of her curiosity and was delighted

with the room and soon began to look upon it as a perfect room. She hadn't expected to get any greater.

She once said, looking at the clutch of disconsolate houses, 'the city was full of strange rumours, but she wouldn't say what they were. If a man is killed, it is an accident of war; but if a woman or a child is killed, it is a barbarous murder and a hundred lives---or a thousand---are sacrificed to avenge it.'

She suddenly heard a sweet-voiced woman. She paused in her sweetest song, and the whole multitude took up the melancholy dirge—a slow, solemn, and mournful piece of song:

'Through all the horror-haunted ways of Hell,

I seek you near and far,

From star to wandering star'

In the gathering twilight, Sarala Devi had felt her way to the open window. She stood there, leaning against the casement; her eyes fixed on the last rosy tints that were fading from the western sky. There was still some of the light on ageing forehead, on her white collar, on her clasped white hands, but all fading slowly away. The suppliant had dragged herself, still on her knees, beside her. Standing near the window, Sarala Devi talked to herself: 'Woman being grown has two ills to fear---Death and Marriage; and of these twain is Marriage the more vile; for in Death we may find rest, but in Marriage, should it fail us, we must find the hell. Who knows that the tempest may not break tomorrow?'

The last red beam of sunlight was creeping higher, suffused Sarala Devi's eyes with something of its glory, flickered, and faded, and went out. The sun had set on the maidan. In the twilight, Sarala Devi's voice sounded pleasantly. Looking at a dirty littered street near the Old People's Home, a note of irritation crept into her voice as she heard filthy street language of squalid slums.

Christmas came and went with its usual family gatherings. Sarala Devi spent the Christmas Day with her co-boarders, who were getting old and crotchety. It had been pleasant to know that Sarala Devi had loved her orphan children sleeping under the open sky. She had loved them almost to the point of adoration where love had more to do with fitting into each other's ways, being a grandmother of her children, depending on each other for social standing and support than with passion.

She muttered: 'Life is hard enough as it is. I'm old enough to decide for myself. It seems pleasant enough to me. I have heard the boarders of this Old People's Home enjoy a high standard of living, and they are happy and get pleasure from what they are doing. I'm sure I'm right.' She felt sure she had forgotten something. An elderly woman, walking past Sarala Devi, sneezed loudly.

'Oh, excuse me. I didn't see you here' said she and left

Looking at her departure, Sarala Devi, moving in a gentle gait and relying on her walking stick. She got back into her room, smiling. She was fast asleep, breathing evenly. She got to know there was a tragic story in every room. That humiliating story had been in train for decades all around the city since British left India.

She woke up as she heard the rumble of distant thunder with heavy trucks kept thundering past the Old People's Home. She laced her fingers behind her head. Her heart was thumping with excitement as thunder crashed in the sky. There was no lightning rod to protect the building from lightning. She lay and listened to those sounds, and could not sleep. Somewhere in the dark recesses of the house a clock struck two.

She thought that she heard whispering voices, and remembering the night that she had listened in the bathroom, and she slipped noiselessly out of bed and tiptoed to the bathroom door. But there were no voices. Only the dry whisper of dead and dying neem leaves that drifted down through the windless air and came to rest on the parched stone of the roof. She had pictured herself as falling asleep and envisioning in her dream a series of allegorical people and events as all other women had.

She was born and brought up in a drowsy village of Bangladesh. She often dredged up memories of her bygone days by deep searching, lying in a bed of Old People's Home. Like all other boarders, she passed the nights in a sustained deep, murmuring, and buzzing sound of bees and mosquitoes. She had the feelings of dejection and hopelessness associated with sadness, inactivity, and difficulty in thinking and concentration. Personal tragedy had drained her of all spirit. Taking a glass of water, she drowned herself in sleep.

Those dreams came when Sleep unlocked the secret heart and set its terrors free to roam through the opened halls of Thought. She seemed to see him in royal form, as erst she had seen it, came with arms outstretched and Love's own light shining in her eyes, with lips apart and flowing locks, and stamped upon her face the look of utter tenderness that she alone could wear. Suddenly she rose and laughed. She learned to love him with all the unspent passion of her aching soul. She felt she had a gloomy and nervous disposition at this age as all other elderly women of Old People's Home. She heard an extremely and unpleasant commotion from the unsteady drunken men getting past the Old People's Home at midnight.

She had not got much sleep last night as the snores of some sleepers broke the silence of the night. She had a vivid, dream look in her eyes about her conjugal life, and she had moved in the dreamy way of a gentleman but failed. She had the dullness and monotony of her everyday life. She hadn't paid attention to what was happening around her. She knew she had been in a state of senile decay. In Old People's Home she finally fell straight into a dreamless sleep. There was no telling what would happen next.

The morning dawned wet and cold. The wind moaned among the bare branches and the draughts whined uneasily along the dark corridors of the awe-inspiring Old People's Home in size and design, and bellied the funereal hangings that draped the walls. The jackets they had worn were too big, even with sweaters underneath. Their faces were deep in shadows lengthened as the sun went down. They were now living under the shadows of fear and suspicion of new strangers wishing to live in Old People's Home. Nourished by hope, the old boarders had sustained heavy losses. Their discussions ranged over a number of topics. As they aged, their memory got worse. No one knew for sure what had happened. They were waiting for death for an undefined period of time at Old People's Home. As she looked out the window of Old People's Home, the edge of the full moon floated over the maidan, and her rays fell upon the Old People's Home where she lived and the temple walls beyond, lighting the visages of the Gods. Looking at the cold light struck the stretch of wide lands, she prayed as she had never prayed before to the Godhead, who is called by many names, and in many forms made manifest.

She retired to bed with hope when to die. Her son's decision to sell the house to a promoter still rankled with her. He had shown a lack of respect for his mother and enjoyed playing tricks on her. He had hardly even dared to speak to her. A series of unpleasant things had happened over a short period of time. In the end she had to get---or rather run---to the Old People's Home. Her mental agony was spreading with alarming rapidly. She closed her eyes and dreamed, because she was looking for something. It was beautiful, with the beauty of a dream, and solemn as the hour after death. Living alone in this Old People's Home, she was angry by shouting loudly at night for a long time.

She looked out the window and saw the people talked in whispers. A man was holding forth excitedly to a dense knot of people as thick as a swarm of bees, and scraps of sentences separated themselves from the sullen murmur of the crowd waiting for the buses. 'The city is out of bounds until further notice…' muttered curses and a man spitting loudly and contemptuously as they passed.

There was seldom much traffic on the roads in the heat of the day during the hot weather. Walking in the maidan was infinitely preferable to the tense atmosphere in the Old People's Home. As the long-limbed and long-bodied cattle were getting back home, they got back home early as the traffic reached its peak between 7 and 10 in the morning. The home-servants were seen wheeling the patents back to their own home. The morning walkers and unassuming neighbours dispersed, melting away into the streets and lanes. Only the unbranded cattle were grazing on the maidan. The field had also been grazed by the sheep.

On the day of his wife's death anniversary, a pigeon-toed old man, leaning on his walking stick, went right to a cremation ground where she had been cremated. He laid a wreath at the altar of his wife's gravestone with much respect in a depressing landscape. The streets were silent as the maidan was deserted. He was strangely silent, sitting there. There was a light background of the gravestone silhouetted against the morning sunlight. As he was about to get back to Old People's Home, looking sullen in a dismally and depressingly dark weather, he stood struck dumb for a moment, for the magic of her voice and the power of her speech stirred him like the rush of music.

He murmured his gracious thanks to his wife and turned to go. He suddenly saw a girl, in a white crinoline and a blue sash, sitting at the gravestone of her departed mother. A pretty creature, barely more than a child, with pale gold ringlets falling on to the sloping shoulders, and one small hand holding a single rose. She was so small and slim and blondly beautiful. It would be unthinkable to have a hand in condemning such a defenceless creature to the life. Between the old man and the small silent child there sprang up a strong bond of sympathy and understanding. He alone got to realize what the child must be suffering in heartache and homesickness, and she sensed the loneliness and the need for affection that lay behind the old man's forbidding exterior and irascible manner.

He stood silent. The morning was cold and windy. Hurrying ranks of clouds streamed endlessly overhead against a luring background of grey skies that failed to show a glimpse of blue sky. The crowd about the cremation was thinning rapidly. As the night was getting darker and darker, some criminals, scratching shallow graves in the iron-hard earth, were trying to cover the corpse of an orphan child.

A lone old woman was standing apart by the nearest old tree, using it as a shelter against the wind and evidently waiting until the major portion of the crowd left the avenue. The wind seemed to strike through her cloth. Something about her attracted his attention, for despite the heavy veil that obscured her features he had the impression that he knew her, or had seen her before. She stood quite still: so still that he suddenly realized when and where it was that he had seen her. It was the woman who had entered the Old People's Home yesterday, and had stood in that same rigid attitude beside a gravestone.

And as he watched, a freakish gust of wind, sweeping about the trunk of the weather-beaten old tree, snatched at the long black veil and whipped it out and above her head, revealing a widow, unguarded face. She had mothered a week-hearted baby that had grown up in her lap for brief days and died in Calcutta at the age of 21. Her week-hearted son was laid to rest by the gravestone of her husband. She had now become mad. She was steadily looking at the gravestones like the shadows of the clouds racing silently over the unheeding earth. He nerved himself to avoid that mysterious woman. On every Monday she used to go to the gravestone to watch her son how he was there.

Looking back at the gravestone of his wife, he said in a low, choked voice, and dropping the level of his eyes, 'Had I not loved you, doubtless you might not have fired me with your flame. You know—none so well—who I am and what my mission is: you know—none so well—that I am alone in Old People's Home. Your beloved son kicked me out of my house. He and his wife made a bargain to tell each other everything. Now I feel life is not a barrel of laughs and a lot of fun.' A question often dawned on him: 'Why do we feel frightened at the time of death?'

His learned friend once answered back to his question. He said: 'As we grow in age, we will go in frustration. We become more miserable. Death comes close and the goal does not come—that is what misery is. That is what frightens us. It is the undying flame that has set all life aglow, yet it must be kindled and rekindled in the abysmal darkness of selfish thoughts, selfish words and selfish deeds.' He got satisfied at his friend's clever, discerning awareness.

He broke in, in his low voice, and with his eyes still fixed upon the ground. He released his breath in an audible sigh and left the place, leaning his hand on the walking stick and groaning in bitterness of spirit. There had been a

heavy and recent fall of earth and stonework from the spot where the roots of the peepul tree had forced their way downwards.

Next day morning, he got to maidan with another old friend for evening walk to get fresh in mind and heart. The sun plunged below the horizon and a sharp sweet smell of wood smoke stole across the maidan, and presently a little chill wind arose, a precursor of the cold winter and a promise of cool nights. He was short and strong, with heavy features. They had lived together for years in the Old People's Home.

He willingly said to his friend: 'Such things are lawful; the sky is a liquid mass pressing round the earth and resting on the elastic pillars of the air, and how above is the heavenly ocean, in which the planets float like ships as they rush upon their radiant way.' When he stood and spoke watching the stars, his friend sat, clasped upon his knee, and watched his face. There were no omens in the skies that night, and the pariah dogs were silent; but the city was not. The city was awake and restless.

'Ah!' his friend broke in at length, 'and so Venus is to be seen both in the morning and the evening sky.'

'Yes, you're right. There is a gloomy cloud of thought. I must find you better. Youth comes but once: why waste it in these musings. It is time to think when we can no longer act. Never talk of woe. Be seated here by me. Let us talk as friend to friend. Tell me how old are you, my friend?' After a long walk, they were seated on a grassy field. Every inch of the maidan was shrouded in uncertainty.

'I have sixty-seven years,' her friend answered, raising her eyes heavenward, 'Sons didn't stand with any the slightest change in the accustomed aspect of things that are daily before their eyes.'

'You're sixteen years junior to me,' said he in a smiling gesture, 'Did you ever love a woman, my friend?'

His friend paused, covering his eyes with his hand. He had said nothing at all for long. He confessed to uneasiness and knew the feel of that sticky wetness of old. He wrinkled his nose expressively.

His friend then said without a trace of doubt, ‘I loved a young girl. There was faith written in those quiet eyes of hers. I can no longer bear my solitude of mind---I must find one with whom I may commune and speak that which lies within my heart. She went, leaving me angered and troubled at heart. I saw her no more that day, but on the day which followed I saw her. She was in a heavy mood, and had no gentle word for me. There was triumph in her eyes, though I knew not over what she triumphed. She sealed the fate of my love. Now I understand a woman doesn't believe in permanence of love. To save the world, we need a total war. This is going to destroy the whole of life on earth. Trees, birds, animals, man---anything living will simply be gone.’

‘What?’ said he anxiously

His friend said tenderly and soothingly, ‘Joyous people don't want war; it is only those who are already dead who would like everybody else to be dead. Love means suffering and pain for oneself and happiness for others. To the giver it is suffering without malice or hatred. To the receiver it is a blessing without obligation. My life was full of pleasure but that caused harm in the end.’

‘That means the path of love is not free from sacrifices. Just as heat and light go hand in hand, so do love and sacrifice. The heart without love is entombed in unending darkness and suffering,’ said he softly.

His eyes prickled with tears, bending his head with a sob burst from the agony of his heart. He stayed silent and did not move as he passed. A few moments later, they left the maidan with a strange and an unpleasant mind.

Several years after, a few boarders had split up; they met again by chance in Old People's Homes. At this crabbed age, they only looked out the windows when yellow leaves, or few, were hanging upon those boughs shaking against the cold wind. The boarders of Old People's Homes, looking out the windows, seemed to have heard the surly, sullen bell of Death. Their smooth and shiny hair had turned into grey. The women of unblessed conjugal life saw the twilight of those days as the sunset faded in the west. It was merely a question of time before their heart collapsed. Two Old People's Homes—one for male and another for women—stood in close proximity to the maidan. The gardener was busy in making trim and neat by cutting the hedges.

A contingent of various old couples huddled together and used to pass off the Old People's Home, chattering and laughing in a superciliously pompous manner, but the elderly boarders kept their shoulders turned to them and no one broke in upon their thoughts, and presently the age-old women drifted back towards the main thoroughfare and they were alone in the moonlight.

Kalpana Devi, senior to all other boarders, was very respectable to them. She felt a deadly excitement. She moved out of concealment and stepped forward to hunt out those unforgotten days around maidan. Then she deliberately stepped on a sodden stick. The stick broke with very little sound. Drawing a long deep breath, she took her seat on a bench lying vacant at the entrance of Old People's Home.

Marriage had troubled her with a rueful disquiet. Triumphantly, she looked forward towards the maidan. The air was heavy with the sounds of vehicles and trucks loaded with goods.

As the sounds of vehicles died away, the echoes still rang in her ears as she walked on with a walking stick, keeping to the cover of trees and walls, taking short-cuts across the compounds of bungalows, and making for the road that led to maidan where her old friends were anxiously waiting for her arrival. She moved with more and more caution as she neared the maidan.

An old friend, aged about 70, shrugged her shoulders and said: 'An hour---two hours---a day. Who knows?' She was smooth-faced and fair to look upon, and with a supple form; but her mouth was cold, and false were her shifting eyes.

She saw Kalpana Devi come near to them and draw a quick breath of relief and said: 'I was delayed, and therefore, I came slowly'---she gave a brief account of that delay. She watched some children loitering about the dusty pavements. They looked distinctly green. She bit her lower lip and put her head down. She looked unaccountably upset, seeking after an unalloyed happiness.

'Assuredly,' said Kalpana Devi unbosoming herself, 'But there is little shade on that road. Our age is like winter weather. At this age, my faith, my tears, and all are mocking at me. A shining gloss of my beauty has died down. Now we say---good night and good rest. At this age, all elderly persons are cowards.'

'Why do you say so?' asked her friend

'Because we are afraid of everything, we simply exist in fear; we go on trembling deep inside. We are just protecting ourselves. Our whole life is a long story of protection, defending. We don't have time how to live and we don't have energy to grow.'

'At this age, all elderly persons believe they are healthy because they are afraid of the medicine, of the physician, of the operation, and of the surgery.'

She gave a bitter smile at them. And then a bird screamed from beyond the bamboo brake---a harsh, grating cry that seemed to echo the gasping screams that had rung in their ears all that cold agonizing afternoon.

She got back to her room of Old People's Home and then became entangled in a succession of crooked and narrow streets, which crossed each other, and meandered at no great distance from the maidan-side. A few yards ahead, she paused to read and informed her that she was near the Old People's Home. The streets were empty, the shops were closed, and the lights were visible only in the second storey of a few dwelling-houses. Finally, she found the Old People's Home, and she got into the room. She tore off her gorgeous garments that her son had given to her on Durga Puja Festival and spat upon them and trod them on the ground. Her son had not talked to her when her son gave her those garments. She had never seen her son again—or the agonizing story of old person goes on. By ignoring the feelings of their parents, sons were only storing up trouble for themselves. Then she put on her feet the sandals of untanned hide.

Her features were separately striking almost to grotesqueness, and the whole face left a deep impression on the memory. The forehead bulged out into a double prominence, with a vale between; the nose came boldly forth in an irregular curve, and its bridge was of more than a finger's breadth; the eyebrows were deep and shaggy, and the eyes glowed beneath them like fire in a cave.

Suffering much relentless, incommunicable grief, and unpleasant experiences had had her feel upset and had aged her enormously. Her small face appeared drained of all colour in the moonlight and she breathed unevenly as though she had been running. Other boarders looked at her in the full moonlight with their own face and felt an odd pain at their heart and a hurt and anger that matched her own. She regarded the strangers with a feeling of distrust. Some boarders got used to paying visit to the local temple.

The crowd about the temple was thinning rapidly, for the keen wind did not encourage loitering. Those who had come or were returning on foot had already set off at a brisk pace, and the carriages that waited to one side of the yew-lined avenue were being filled and driven away. They were not as happy as a big sunflower as they were before. Happiness was to them was like sunshine; it is made up of very little beams. Days went by after disappointment. They were lonely, missed their friends more than ever, and their meetings with them were too infrequent to be looked on as more than isolated adventure. At this age, they looked at each other in a suspicious glance.

The fairground was surrounded by the booths of sweetmeat-sellers, hucksters, and there was plenty to entertain the idle: jugglers, acrobats, fire-eaters, a sad and ragged performing bear, snake-charmers, and fortune-tellers. Some morning walkers, with a surge of interest, got to know their fate that unpredictably determined events and issues favourably or unfavourably. The old ones got back home in irritably sullen and churlish mood, knowing their calamitous fate. An old person felt the blood surging into his face. Remorse was

their daily portion. They tried forgetting those disbelieving days like the swift shadows of Noon.

The whole town was quite different from any other town in India. The town was provided well with buses, trams, and major road links. It smelt of all sorts of things they had not smelt before; as the morning walkers walked down the maidan amid the sun and shadow with the dust playing in whorls between the rundown houses and multi-storeyed buildings, their nostrils were assailed then with the odour of untended refuse from squalid pavements.

Some elderly women standing from the balcony of Old People's Home noticed a little girl came running across the pavement. Among them an elderly woman recognised her. She poignantly reminded her only little daughter who had died when her father had been at war as a soldier in World War II. Her eyes flooded with tears. She steadily looked at the little girl. Her little hands and legs were pricked and scratched by the stubble and the sunburn lay on her rosy cheeks like a lawny web. The abandoned children were playing ludo, squatting on the dusty floor of the pavement. It was a potentially explosive environment. The little girl was glad to see her father. Sitting in a squat, she clung to his side, and talked away without a stop. She gathered twigs, leaves and corn ears and sat down beside her father.

'Daddy, play corn ears with me!' said the little girl feeling a ringing, stinging, and thrilling sensation. A huge bunch of kids came stampeding down the pavements and gathering around the girl.

She screwed up her eyes and began singing in her thin voice:

'Gather the twigs and corn ear,

Speak the word

And we shall hear!'

A mile outside the city of Calcutta some areas lay silent and deserted. Here and there a bungalow seemed to still burned and creeping figures still slunk between the silent houses, searching for any loot that might have been

overlooked during the day-long orgy of murder and robbery as the British rule in India was going on. But as the evening shadows lengthened, the dead who lay about the city filled even the scum of the city with uneasiness and superstitious fear.

The age-old morning walkers got to the maidan to have a walk for pleasure and for exercise to relieve the boredom of loneliness. Their conversations sometimes laced with sarcasm and lame racist jokes. Some walkers kept trimming their physical condition by jogging in a less hygienic area of maidan, because they had got a supportive experience of the dangers of morning walk. They saluted the orphan children before leaving the maidan and prayed for the salvation of the orphan children.

The frightening feeling of loneliness and insecurity among them had been so familiar a part of their livelihood that they could not express anything with other while walking in the maidan. The wide maidan was a great relief for them to be able to talk to someone. An old man was seen wishing to say something in a low angry voice but he couldn't as he gritted his teeth against the pain. The kittens were seen enjoying a roll in the morning sunshine.

The old trees--standing out in sharp relief against the blue sky--creaked and groaned in the mild wind blowing from the south. The road lay empty on either side of Old People's Home but they could see men move before the toll-house. The city was in shambles after the World War II. And the economy was in a state of great disorder. It lessened the stability of their faith in livelihood as the people saw through the hollowness, the sham, and the silliness of the empty pageant.

The sun touched the rim of the maidan, and a cuckoo called from the thickets behind the morning walkers. A few stray dogs were looking up at them interestingly. They didn't know what was happening behind their gloomy face. Some dogs came close to a wailing elderly woman, looking steadily at her. They couldn't apprehend why she had to do that. Many stories of excitement and adventure often set in the past around maidan. Romance is always in the air.

Even the age-old sex-workers, getting worse in health and cunningly concealed their old profession, got to the maidan to get fresh air at morning. They thought morning walk would help them feel fresher and fitter. They were seen sneakily walking together by the side of maidan.

A senior sex-worker, Latika Devi, at 70, said in a low voice, 'I didn't get much sleep last night. I need to get some sleep. Ever and again I open my door and look out on the darkness, my friends! I can see nothing before me; I wonder where my path lies! At this age, I feel we're all fools. The first chapter of fools is to esteem themselves wise. But…' Fatigued by the last night's chores and wearied of constant arguing with them, she was unable to continue. She rested her chin upon her hand and the cloud of thought gathered in her eyes.

Her beauty had once surpassed description as she was in Sonagachi. All customers had given a preferential rating to get into her room. Even the purse-proud age-old persons would have been fortunate if they had happened to get into her room. She got frightened in an exciting way of those of spine-chilling days in Sonagachi.

All remained silent. The moist earth steamed under the sun, and the swollen branches of the trees were velvety-black. The odours of earth and damp branches were pungent and thrilling. There was a fraught silence all over the maidan. Latika Devi, looking fresh, bright and attractive, felt singing was quite the best way to get fresh in the morning. She felt a tremble of excitement run through her and then she started to sing in this fresh morning:

'We'll walk together with all

Along roads, both narrow and wide'

Other plump sex-workers stared out intently with an avid happy smile. They found themselves marching in step with the song with their fat flabby legs. Whenever they were under an emotional strain they kept silent. She buttoned up her jacket and began slowly and carefully combing her hair. The years' experience at red-light areas had shown how happy they had been there.

Someone suddenly said in a fierce whisper (pulling her hand): 'There! There! A tall and bald-headed old person, holding a walking stick in his worn-out hand, is walking closely to us. He is looking at us with shrieks of fiendish laughter. He seems to have been our regular customer. Am I right, madam?'

Looking at him, they were convulsed with laughter. Her quirk sense of humour was characteristically British.

Turning off her face, Latika Devi observed him with a stereoscopic vision. She thought with compassionate and loving amusement. She murmured, looking at him: 'This is going to be a hard and decisive time for me. It's perhaps the hardest and most decisive in my life. All customers in Sonagachi are psychologically as unsteady as shadow. He seems to be extremely clever and complicated. Who is that vicious old man—a conspirator or a traitor?'

Her colleagues saw a tremor run across her cheeks and eyebrows, and a tensity settle about her temples and the corners of her eyes. The whole of his figure and even the small tuft of hair on the crown of his head wore an injured expression. She looked at him with the affectionate superiority of a woman. Her feelings about the matter didn't seem to figure at all and not figure high on her list of customers. He was constantly smiling with an impish look. Different kinds of people from overly societies were brought into casual association in maidan. Latika Devi knew them well. Looking at her toil-worn hands, she looked back over her past days when she had stepped into the forbidden doors of Sonagachi.

Recollecting the sublime confidence of her youth, Latika Devi said, 'Yes, my sister, I have recognised him. He is Ganesh Mondal, to be sure, he is also very sex-monger. He is a manifold liar for many reasons. He came to Sonagachi at midnight as a jackal which rushed prowling through the land, as a grim lion that frequents hidden paths, as a powerful bull with sharpened horns.' She paused for a moment. Raising her pale face, she looked at the man standing off a century-old banyan tree. She further said:

'He's that stupid fellow. How selfish, stupid, and ungrateful can he be! I recognise him by the hollows in his cheeks grew deeper and the wild helpless

resentment in his eyes increased. He changed himself by artful means so as to serve his purpose and masked his real purpose at Sonagachi. He's neither a conspirator nor a traitor. So far as I know none of five children was born at the same time to the same mother. Days come and ages pass, and it is ever he who moves my heart in any a name, in many a guise, in many a rapture of joy and sorrow.' She began to weep with convulsive catching of the breath. She then breathed through an obstructed nose with a sniffing sound. All others came close to her and consoled her.

'How do you say so, madam,' asked a middle-aged sex-worker, raising her quizzical eyebrows. She threw out a remark that confounded other sex-workers.

'It's your implausible idea,' said Latika Devi, 'Conspirator or traitors are like moths, which eat the cloth in which they are bred; like vipers, which gnaw the bowels where they are born; like worms, which consume the wood in which they are engendered. A lot of conspirators and traitors were said to seek shelter in Sonagachi from the police during the British rule. They don't know a rational understanding of the laws of nature can quell impossible desires. Knowingly or unknowingly, some prostitutes had to protect them too much from unpleasant and difficult experiences. Do you know even the freedom fighters had led a sheltered life in Sonagachi? Let's drop the matter.' After her divorce Latika Devi had resorted to her old profession as a prostitute.

'I heard it. Give me a straight-out answer, please. Are you sure about that stranger coming close to us?' asked her colleague with a singular feeling of disaster, looking at her with a round-eyed look in surprise. Other sex-workers felt worried at his capricious and unpredictable wandering as some other morning walkers did all around the maidan. Their morning walk filled with strange sights. Straightway the clouds began to part.

'Yes, of course. He is that nonsense leaning on his walking stick. Not only that but so many vile persons walking in the morning get used to taking a step towards the doors of Sonagachi at midnight. Sunday is not our only day off. Sinners have no Sunday. We take this profession on a day-to-day basis. All men are bad, and they reign in their badness. Those are all our customers. I suppose

that the fate of all sinners is loneliness,' said Latika Devi gaily and on the same note of pleased surprise that was in her smile. It was a pleasant smile; the smile an actress might have employed to indicate pleasurable smile. Other sex-workers, getting close to her, asked: 'Why are you smiling?' They got to feel that his presence had made their morning walk worse.

She thought for a moment and said in a low voice, 'As the caterpillar chooses the fairest leaves to lay her eggs on, so those morning walkers got to Sonagachi to feel the fairest joys of happiness and delight. They got in very late at night. In a sense Ganesh Mondal has felt himself to be a sinner all his life. Don't be so feeble! My sister,' said Latika Devi, keeping an apprehensive look in all directions.

'How did you learn it?' said an elderly sex-worker by a strong and urgent desire, looking steadily at her. Other sex-workers were looking for a friendly ear.

Latika Devi was deeply ashamed of her profession. 'I'm ashamed that I'm lucky to meet with some learned persons who got used to come to my room at night. I have learnt it from them. Ideas that have engrossed the minds of scholars for generations make me a knowledgeable prostitute. Happy as he is, there is something missing. The cold early night was a new world, moonless dark. In Bengal the women are not cowed and relegated to harems, as in the Muslim countries. Here they laugh and are happy and free. The Hindu women are wonderfully tolerant and all the harshness and cruelty of Hinduism has come out of their festivals.' She said in a throaty voice and smiled, and others smiled back.

All other ageing sex-workers got pleased at her thoughtful but reasonable point of view.

Without conceit, she got to know that there was a difference between her and most of the morning walkers whom she had met at Sonagachi. They moved quicker and thought quicker. Often in conversation Latika Devi had found herself running on ahead like a child before its grandparents, coming back to

pick them up, then running on again. She took up her bag, felt out a handkerchief and blew her nose loudly.

The distance was a mere fifteen yards from them. She recollected the scene that had taken place between them on the day of her arrival in Sonagachi---a renowned red-light area in Calcutta---and the arguments Ganesh Mondal had used to persuade her, and she slyly and cautiously continued the discourse with a secret smile. The music of those unforgotten years sounded again in her soul.

Suddenly it was cold, a cold layer of air descending as a mantle upon their shoulders, and Latika Devi drew her woolen stole round her. History and Geography were near, talking to each other and greeting people here and there, tossing their heads and laughing and glancing around.

In the beginning, their attitude toward old haggard had not been planned. It had just happened. It was impossible to avoid him and equally impossible to act toward him as if nothing had occurred. The alternative was to try to ignore him. His reaction had been unexpected and had at first given them a bitter satisfaction. The sex-workers, threatened by his presence, left the maidan hurriedly, walking fast past the Old People's Home and making their ways through narrow alleys. They had got a sudden sharp feeling of excitement in maidan.

A long silence fell between them. The day was unusually cold and sunny for the time of year, with the temperature in the nineths. The month might have been December were it not for the angle of the sunshine slanting through the trees and casting the long shadows of houses and Old People's Homes across the dusty road.

Having been neglected for years in their own home, they looked sullen and silent in glum and grave. In a lonely room they cried with despair making low weak noises. Their appearances looked to be neglectful. Most of them had hidden the true situation and pretended that everything was going well. To think of them was to sink into clutching quicksands of panic and horror. They

were not given enough care and attention. The elderly persons tried blooming like the smouldering lilies unconsumed.

Old men and women, bending from the waist and bringing their heads down to their knees, were seen walking slowly and unsteadily with their walking sticks to get enough fresh air from the stultifying effects of work that never varied. Mental depression and anxiety had pulled them down. As the time went on they grew more and more impotent.

Some purse-proud men, having had their pet dogs stuffed, got to maidan for a walk so that they couldn't be harmed by the stray dogs loitering about the maidan, catching a secret smile while talking to others. They came to appreciate and understand the pulsing life of the maidan. Sometimes there were fifteen to twenty tea-sellers, awaiting their orders; then one by one as they received they would slip away to their own house. The truant boys and girls of toileted beauty, sitting behind the huge branches of fresh coconut trees, were bubbling like a tea-kettle beginning to boil and flirting with each other with a flush of eagerness.

The Old People's Home of old persons stood by itself in nine-hundred square-feet. Breakfast was served between 8 and 9 a.m. Never did their religious faith separate one from the other. The management served wonderful meal to more than twenty boarders. Friendly and helpful were their neighbourly relations. They looked at each with a neighbourly gesture. The courtyard was shaded by old trees. Several buildings prevented direct sunlight reaching into the rooms. They were breathing a small amount of air each time. A market in close proximity was in the shadow of a bank. Shafts of fear were always running through them as they felt the footsteps of Death behind them. It was their worst agonies not knowing where their grandsons and grand-daughters were. They looked bewildered and, for some strange reasons, a little frightened.

The boarders, driven out by their sons, never ever felt proud of living in the houses. Their dignity was losing ground. They heard their sons' masterful buccaneering chuckle to be followed by a little high-pitched laugh and deceiving look. As they had left their houses crying, their sons' sardonic smile went slower and deeper, and subsided to a less throaty smile. Most of them wouldn't have thought it possible; they wouldn't know what to expect from their sons. 'Too soon...not decent...How dare you?' They were barely able to stand on with their walking-sticks. They were aware of everything that was happening around them.

Most of them had chosen death at this age, because they got ashamed of this shrinking and fading, of what time would do to their fiction of magnificence, time like the river would wear away their pain of defeats and broken promises, time and the river would blur their faces as a giant incubus, time and the river would mute the vibrations of their voice upon their heart...tomorrow the city would ferment with new disasters, the paper vendors would raise their voices to the pitch of hysteria, the crowds would gather to discuss the news full of yellow journalism; the trains, buses, and other vehicles would carry away the cowards....

They eventually set foot in Old People's Home for every possible event. They had never been here before. They felt the cold more than the young. Greatly daring, an old widower, aged about seventy-six, turned the handle of door and pushed it a few inches open. The room had all been cleared and freshly aired. Looking all around the room, he said to himself, 'Never in all my life have I expected and seen such a horrible thing.'

His eyes flooded with tears. Wiping out his tears with his torn handkerchief, he suddenly felt a faint sweet smell of femininity came to his nostrils. It thrilled him at this age; everything that was dainty and pure and untouchable went with that smell, the essence of womanhood and beauty and grace.

He felt a kind of wonder singing inside him. At this age, he was waiting for a distant, unknowable divine power when to die at this Old People's Home. He was a cancer patient and forcibly driven out by his sons and daughters-in-law. His defeat to his only son was unexpected. Now he was enjoying his new-found freedom at this Old People's Home. Sitting nearest to the window, he visualized his wife's face as he talked to her. How first it would be dark and angry with that black fire burning in her eyes and then gradually the anger would go away as he talked until finally she reached up and touched his cheek like she used to do before, and she looked at him with that funny soft smile he could never quite explain and she'd say as if he were a little boy, 'It's all right, my darling. Can you meet me at the barricade, my darling? I'll be waiting there for you.'

'What! It's at the barricade! Where is it? Since we came into this crying world, we all have been waiting for someone or something.' He said to be slightly surprised with a curious expression.

He heard a crackly voice saying, 'It's that barricade from where no man returns. At this age it's our cracking destiny. Don't waste time worrying about our son's behaviour.' He started sobbing uncontrollably, recollecting his conjugal life. He couldn't stop crying.

The door made a noisy click as he closed it, and he stood in the darkness of the passage for some seconds listening to the beating of his own heart. Faintly he smelt the sweet smell of femininity from the neighboring building. He closed the windows. He had a vivid dream about his conjugal life while he was asleep: 'She smiled and sat down at the bench beside him. He put the perfume at her ears and throat. She put her arm around me and pressed me close and tight. It's sweet. It is wonderful perfume.' she said with a jerk of her head towards the verandah outside, 'let's go out and get something to eat anyway.'

He woke up finding himself alone in his bed. He got down from the bed to drink water. The water was unexpectedly cold and the churning wake sucked him down. He felt apprehensive as she looked at the corner of the room which was damp where the roof had leaked. Various stores and restaurants stood off the Old People's Homes. It was six o'clock in the morning. It was cool; the air felt good and fresh. He withdrew a hanger on. It was plaid wool, orange and yellow stripes making interlocked squares on a green base.

Looking all around the room, he cried aloud and spoke to himself: 'It's like a desert island. The older I grow, the more I see my mistake. The world's a snare, make no mistake of it. And everybody is marooned in this desert island.

Everybody's different like the trees in a forest. Some's crooked; some's straight. Some's healthy; some's got moss on them. Some'll stand any storm; others will fall at the first puff. Some's got fruit that's good to pick; some hasn't. And I can't tell. Not the cleverest person in the world can tell what's behind a face. They think they can, but they can't.'

He laughed; anyone as old as he should have been amused at the perverted vitality of the dream. He looked pale, with deep shadows under his eyes. He thrust his lower lip out purposefully and made his voice as deep as he could: 'Father said when he was away, I was to look after you.'

One grey lock of hair was falling over his forehead and he had set his jaw in a faithful imitation of his father.

Silence fell. His disjointed allegories were too much for his misfortune. Eyes pricking, he watched the shadowy light grow in the east, slowly gaining ascendency until it penetrated into other rooms, showing up new outlines of disordered chairs and tables, whitening a pile of broken crockery, driving before it the dismal defeated light of the flickering street light. Unnoticed, his face had also emerged wan and bloated and strained.

He got into the room allotted for him. He lay back in bed breathing out his relief slowly from between closed teeth. He rubbed his eyes, his mind tearing off the fetters of nightmare even more slowly than it had done four nights earlier when his two sons had driven him out of the house. A few mornings ago, he had taken his seat with his sons while a life ebbed away unhurriedly

Day was coming, Clouds high in the sky had begun to flush. They reflected a terra-cotta stain upon the opal blue. Some birds had begun to wheel and cry. The night he had was another unpleasant dream. After half an hour, the sky was clear. The sunlight falling through the narrow window lit up the room greyly.

A lonely old woman---Kalpana Devi having a dark view of the future---was standing apart by the Old People's Home of old women, using it as a shelter against the cold draught of wind. She had witnessed the yeasty periods in freedom movement, remembering yards of facts and figures of British rule. Never had she yielded too easily in any argument of British officials. She had always been young at heart. The memory of that dream crept into her mind like a thief. So vivid had been the dream that even now she could almost see their furtive glance at her. She felt foolish and a failure. Fear of loneliness and mental anguish seeped through her being. She had spent many lonely nights at home watching the silence of the nights.

It gave her a cool dull smile. She was barely 80 years old and--- most senior to all other dwellers of Old People's Home of women--- looking forward to the darkest reaches of the maidan, not receiving, reflecting, and radiating light. She had lost her looks, and could hardly read a vernacular newspaper. She was worriedly looking at the several dilapidated houses--built up during the British regime—which were moved bodily to new sites. She felt aggressive, clenching her tapping fingers impatiently. Everything, at this stage, had driven her to despair. Some things happened without any cause that she couldn't understand.

She opened the window and looked down on the ill-kept slum areas. Children were seen hanging around the dusty pavements because there was nowhere for them to play. They were treated like second citizens of India. She felt worried as she watched the shabbily-looking slum-dwellers, wearing run-down clothes, were loitering about the pavements for their own needs. She got to feel about her husband.

'My husband is a fine musician,' said she often proudly, 'He played the sitar and was studying the Bhagavad Gita, the Song of God, to improve the spirit of love in his music. For without love, nothing is beautiful.' She had loved him the way he wanted to be loved. She was nice and wifely to him then. She remembered her deep sleep, a dreamless saturation.

There was a clear peal of thunder, and the soft splash of rain outside, on the sputtering gravel, on the cars and jeeps, on the slum-dwellers. People standing out the balcony came into the rooms. The downward glitter of water lasted only a few minutes, freshness wafted in, the sitar played, the sun came through again.

'Rain, before the bridegroom comes,' said Kalpana Devi. 'It is a good omen.' Along the road--winding and swaying from side to side in a rumour of wind-swept music and laughter--the bridegroom's procession came like a short and colourful snake towards the house.

Kalpana Devi was slow in awakening and then walking down the verandah, where the shadow of a loitering servant lay long upon the marble-stone ; her dreams of greatness and magnificence were heavy on her body like garments but the face she opened to the dawn was the face of innocence, as every man presents innocence to the new day. She got into the bathroom to take a warm bath to soothe tense, tired muscles. After having a bath, she felt calmer. Having a warm bath removed her unpleasant feeling.

Kalpana Devi had wakened to find herself alone in bed, sat up to see herself in the large mirror, startled by the mosquito net, green. She slipped out through the back door and was rather upset to find a thin mist lying over the maidan. In this life she had to do what she meant to do or else shrivel up in self-contempt. She rushed downstairs and came to the balcony, steadily looking at the blue sky. The tireless wind---the clean wind of night---sang on, fraught with ringing, rocking souls. The sound of wind was sad and old and impersonal, as if it spoke of creation and decay. She got back to her room.

She noticed that the shadows on the wall were still, but the reflections of the lights on the floor played on the surface like a ghost's carnival. The candles flickered more than usual, or was it her anxiety? She had no physical fear. She feared truth; she feared to confront her motives, feared to face, to understand, to examine in the realm of feelings and thoughts, but she didn't fear to act, she didn't fear physical danger. She waited for the evening. Every evening was as shocking as stinging shame to the dwellers of Old People's Home.

The stars blazed like wedding rings in the darkness and, falling on her, were entangled in her grey hair and extinguished in her tousled head. The loitering moon crept out from behind the clouds and lingered on her. The misty moon loitered about the sky like a beggar woman.

The night-times at Old People's Homes were the worst of all. The boarders retired to bed at eleven. It was a large double-bed, and she climbed into bed. Once in it she was suddenly beset by loneliness and bereavement. Years ago she had slept in a bed like this, but beside her there had been the warmth and softness and all-embracing guardianship of her husband. It had been sufficient for him to be, to exist unthinkingly, in the aura of that loving, understanding, comforting protection. As her husband had died, she was alone in an alien world of Old People's Home.

Kalpana Devi closed the door noisily, sleeping solidly for seven hours. She was filled with longing to hear her husband's voice again as she stood before a broken mirror. She felt worried, looking at her longish hair getting greyer and greyer. She was longing to see him again, and she knew he no longer lived in this world.

She would lie there, defenseless as the flood of memories surged through her, for in this bed he had loved her, his dear hands and his strong body had roused and satisfied her desire. Sometimes she had wakened and watched her beloved husband as he slept and thanked God for the fact of him; for what he was and what he had given her. Unfortunately, he had sacrificed his life in Indo-China war in 1962 and was a martyr to the cause of freedom. One of the bullets had lodged in his chest. Looking at the picture of her well-built up husband, she was very much proud of her husband and stared at him in disbelief. At this age, she often felt irregular heartbeat. She was alone in an alien world.

There were times when she remembered her husband's first smile, the ironic smile of the Indian which came from afar like the echo of an ancient Indian smile at the beginning of Mayan worlds; the earthy walk issued from bare footsteps treading paths into the highest mountains of the world, into the most immune lakes and impenetrable forests.

In her dream of her husband, she returned to the origins of the world. She had kissed the Indian princes of her childhood fairytales. She had plunged with love and desire into the depths of ancient races, and sought heights and depths and magnificence. Alone at night, after the torments of her life, she got to feel that it was real, it was life, it was heightened life, and that happiness was a mediocre ideal, held in contempt by the poets, the romantics, the artists—alone at night when she acknowledged to herself that everything was doomed.

She felt whoever was without flaw; whoever understood, whoever contained an inexhaustible flow of love was god the father whom she had lost in her childhood. She believed that World War II and troubles had heightened the flavour of life that scenes were necessary to the climax of desire, like fire, suddenly in touching the bottom of the abysmal loneliness in the Old People's Home.

Kalpana Devi got as far as the back door with a book of her wedding pictures in one hand and a walking stick in the other. As she closely watched the pictures of wedding, she began crying aloud and found herself leaning faintly against the table while the agony of anguish and loneliness flushed over her again. The sobs went on steadily for a long time. She went up to a terrible pitch and the tremendous outpouring of damned-up emotion caught at her heart until she had to squeeze her fists together to keep her own tears from starting again. It was quite dark before the sobbing stopped altogether. She often said to her colleagues in good-natured banter:

'I'm like a hackneyed car to go for a servicing centre that was too badly damaged to be repaired.' She lay on the bed wide-eyed and wakeful and for the first time in days managed, by a desperate and sustained effort, not to cry.

'Oh God, teach me how to live without him to the last days of my life! Oh God, we are born like a momentary fly to flutter, buzz around, and die. To fear love is to fear life.' She said inelegantly, raising her face heavenward, in the sheer direness of the situation.

The night was hot and very still. So still that every small sound of all the small sounds that went to make up silence separated itself from its fellows, and emphasized that stillness. Only the dry whisper of dead and dying neem leaves that drifted down through the hot, windless air and came to rest on the parched stone of the roof. The noise of the flapping punkah had irritated her, and she had sent the punkah coolie away, saying that she could have slept better without it. But when he had gone she wished that she could call him back, for the sweltering, breathless stillness that had closed down upon the room with the cessation of the slow away of the punkah had been worse than the nerve-racking monotony of that creek and flap.

She was very upset at what to her husband was just a throwaway remark. Her face stiffened, and there were suddenly two white patches at the corners of her mouth. She laughed with a disillusioned jowly face. Her hand dropped and she stepped back. Dread, implacable, passion-drenched, her song soared through the night in Old People's Home. She began to sing:

She'll not forget; she will come with caresses;

She will embrace, with a love that is endless,

Laying her bride's wreath upon her dark tresses!

'How is it? Brilliant!' she muttered, 'You've been brilliant.'

She looked happier as she sang. Her gentle tune was a salve to her spirit, making her feel calm and relaxed. The song flew on like the waters of eternity, washing all away, giving birth to all. The effortless freshness and spontaneity of her singing would put her into the front rank of popular singers, not only of the present time but of any time.

There was no air, only a drifting mist which had to be breathed in wet and breathed out in a finer form as if the moisture had been refined into steam. The night received her like an over-attentive and slightly sinister friend. For a long time she was too preoccupied with her thoughts to feel any sense of her own isolation. She knew in her heart that this was only a moral quibble which really evaded nothing; she had never used it before in any serious matter.

Next day morning, she, having had a mouthful of water from an earthen jar of water, came downstairs. The sun rose as she stood before her household deity. She sat looking out across the maidan beyond, while every blade and spear of grass flashed and glittered with dewdrops, and the morning mists lifted in veil after veil so that the maidan seemed to unroll itself. Doves were seen cooing among the branches of the banyan tree, and a flight of ducks whistled overhead, making for the river, the Ganges, that lay miles. Turning her face back off the window, she paid attention to her prayer. She folded the quiet hands across her chest, closing her eyes:

'May the Lord God, abundant in mercy, keep me with the true speech, and lead me to the perfect path. I'm getting really paranoid delusions what other boarders of this Old People's Home say about her. Diseases are paralleled by an increase in age. Oh great and glorious God, I beseech you with humility, make the earth comfortable to this your servant's side, and raise your soul to me, and with you may I find mercy and forgiveness. I know death is as certain as that my shadow will follow me.'

The murmured words had awakened a soft echo in the shuttered brick-walled room, and when they ceased there was only the buzz of the swarms of flies once more. Branches dripped high overhead and somewhere near water were running in a ditch.

Her small tattered shoes were stretched towards the warmth, toes touching. Her mouth fell slowly open. She heard someone talking downstairs. She looked at them directly in the eye, standing head-on in front of them. 'Who're you in Old People's Home?' asked she. Her voice was quite unnatural. She said again and urgently: 'Get out right now from here!'

'We'll go now, grand-mother,' said they nervously. A few minutes later they left the place singing a romantic filmy song.

The widowers, having been driven out by their sons and having taken a safe haven in Old People's Homes, were seen hanging around the maidan looking for a new way of life---a solitary instance of beauty in the midst of revolting but repulsive environment. After the death of their wives, the widowers had been caught in the net of suspicious circumstances under the supervision of their sons and daughters-in-law. A few of them were seen staring at the sky in vacant eyes for long. They seemed to have been after the honeycomb but had forgotten the bees.

The boarders of Old People's Home found loneliness boring at home. They got used to waking early in the morning, getting themselves alone in these rooms as the cocks began crowing, crows cawing, kittens mewing inside the rooms, and birds chirping. A few of them spent the morning padding about the lawn of Old People's Home in their slippers. They looked back on as being better than the present. They sat all day long doing nothing, feeling that 'We're here today, tomorrow, and the day after; but the next, we're off!' The city was spread out beneath them in its entire splendor.

That lonely woman, Kalpana Devi, born of a middle-class family and bent down in age, was steadily looking for someone to come. Sadananda Manna, security guard of Old People's Home, got puzzled at the sight of their senior dweller. He came and said soothingly, 'Why are you standing here, grandmother?' Feeling the fresh air having brought a healthy glow to her wrinkled cheeks, she felt a pleasure of pride. There were raindrops like a spangle of moonstones on her dark hair, and the cold air had whipped a glow of colour into her pale cheeks.

'Oh yeah, I'm waiting for my son who comes to see his mother on every Sunday,' said she looking at him in half-hidden eyes, 'my son hasn't come here for over two months to see his mother. He seems to have made me persona non grata with everyone of my colleagues in this Old People's Home. Caterpillars change into butterflies, leaves change colour in autumn, the wind changes its direction, and everyman changes his tune, clothes, shoes, and address, and old age changes into total chaos. However every son changes his mind after marriage to look after his old parents. Do you understand what I say, Sadananda?' He anxiously stared at her and felt that she was getting very depressed, anxious and tired.

'Yes, I do,' he said in a nervous voice. His hair was tousled and his face was dirty.

Scanning and eyeing each passer-by anxiously and suspiciously, she said, 'I can recognize my son by his walk in this crowded city. I don't know what happens to him? Death draws near to me and His shape is Silence. He enters at my heart, enters with a sense of numbing cold, but my brain is still alive. I know that I'm drawing near the confines of the Dead. Good Lord, what have you done to my lot! Well, this is it! Wish me luck.' She said rapidly and almost inaudibly in an undertone.

She said uniformly like the gentle sound of a stream flowing over stones. She spoke in a confused way that was difficult for him to understand. Her excruciating words had sharpened up his thoughts.

Her agonizing words were like a dried flower. The colour was faded and the perfume gone. The void left by three dwellers' death last week made the Old People's Home gloomy.

'Would I help you take you back to your room, grandmother,' he asked calmly and thoughtfully

She flushed with pleasure. She glanced over his shoulder. He was of a cheerful and gregarious disposition and always ready to enter into conversation with all the dwellers. She felt the mixture of invisible odorless, tasteless gases that surrounded the earth.

'Wait for a few minutes more,' said she, looking at the passers-by with a steady eye, 'Can you tell me why today and tomorrow will be yesterday, Sadananda?'

Her voice descended into the depths of her morose. She suddenly raised her mournful eyes and her eyebrows as if to say, 'There! There! My son is coming, there he is; he disclaims all responsibility. The worst enemies of old age are brute facts. It's a penalty for my being a mother!' Keeping her hand on the walking stick, she lifted her other hand into the air in dismay from her imprisoned soul of fact. She then grabbed his arm to stop herself from falling.

'Don't worry, grand-mother, 'said Sadananda, patting her shoulder delicately, 'I agree with you, as it happens. There's something not quite right here, grand-mother.' A sudden sharp apprehension and fear dawned on her.

Realising that her son wouldn't come, she decided to get back to her room, wailing and weeping, and making a deep, murmuring soul, 'All are selfish in a wilderness of this crying world. I'm a burden to my son. All flowers don't bloom up in a garden. Some flowers go to red-light areas or some to wedding houses, or to burial ground. All kinds of belief are fear-oriented. The one permanent emotion in old age is fear---fear of the unknown, the complex, and the inexplicable.'

Sadananda looked puzzled at her answer and said: 'How can we believe?'

'It's very easy to answer,' said she, 'unless you have heard reality as it is, there is no possibility of having faith. Faith does not come by fear, faith does not come by greed, and faith comes only through experience.'

Sadananda remained silent and spoke to himself: 'In old age, the eyes of elderly women, like a shattered mirror, multiply the images of their sorrows.'

Rubbing her eyes wearily, she paused for a moment, and then said: 'Glory to God in the highest. God knows there is risk in refusing to act till the facts are all in. I feel a sense of personal freedom here in this Old People's Home. That it is spiritual rather than a material freedom doesn't seem to matter. All people are born in good health, but none died healthily. Night and day their steps sound by my door.' She looked relaxed and elegant, closing her eyes.

Opening her eyes, Kalpana Devi looked at the one who remained with her. Kalpana Devi sat down and pointed at the chair, for her to do the same, but she, having lost her husband and son, got mad and remained standing. The mad woman leaned one elbow on the mantel; her hand fell upon a little ornament that her husband had bought for her. She turned it over and over in her fingers. The mad woman stood without talking, and watched her go into the bedroom. The mad woman disappeared and went right to maidan. There she sat at the feet of a tree, looking vacantly and uncomprehendingly at the house on the evening of the wedding. She tried to slough off the memories of the past.

Kalpana Devi woke up early in the morning as all others boarders did so. The brightening light beat against her closed eyelids and the grey fog in her brain lifted and shredded away like mist drifting off the river, the Ganges, in the early morning, and slowly and almost imperceptibly the pain in her heart lessened and peace took its place. She had the habit of slouching around the morning reading the book of poems for their expressiveness, lyricism, and formal grace. She had poetical ideas about life. She felt but didn't see the first dazzling rim of the sun lip the edge of the far horizon.

Sadananda, security guard of Old People's Home (women), was doing his duty. None had slipped through his vigilant eyes. Whenever he smacked of any doubtful movement near the entrance and heard any harsh and unpleasantly metallic voice, he rushed forward and said politely, 'Don't make a noise here. Don't behave in a silly and annoying way. Don't transform yourself from a dew bride to an ill-mannered, murderous courtesan. The present society is callously neglectful of the elderly persons. Here stands the Old People's Home. Stop messing around here and leave the place now.'

When he started looking at his watch, he suddenly heard a melodious tune of a woman singing to a sitar from somewhere of the Old People's Home (women); the words were quite clear in the quiet evening. For half a minute he stopped in his stride and considered turning back. He stood quiet, listening to the vibrant tunes. The song seemed to have an optimistic view of life. The song of unforgotten years sounded in his soul in unaffected, natural manner. The song was a continual source of delight to him. He tried to guess the meaning of the words from the song.

'...Wae nadani ki waqt-e-marg

Yhi sabit hua

Khwab tha Jo kuch ki dekha Jo

Suna afsani tha'

(Alas we were all ignorant, and only at the time of our death was it proved that whatever we had seen was all a dream, and whatever we had heard was a short tale.') His shining smile brightened his face.

Sadananda brightened up at his words of encouragement. He, steadily looking at the upper-storeyed room, demanded impatiently and ungraciously, 'Who's that woman singing a Ghazal, grand-mother?'

'The song you hear from somewhere was being sung by Nani...' said she

'It's Nani! Who is she?' interrupted Sadananda wearily. The sound of his laboured breathing tore at her heart. He put up a hand and felt his bruised and swollen jaw tenderly. He turned and faced her. She still said nothing. He was waiting for her reply. She unpinned her crisp grey hair and let it fall about her shoulders; then she began to brush it with a measured sweep which she often found soothing.

'Nani—a Muslim woman of seventy-nine years old—used to sing that. She was hailed from Uttar Pradesh. She has taken the last refuge of old age in this Old People's Home. It is a song that was sung long before the battle of Plassey was fought,' said she smiling sweetly, gesturing at the upper-storied room, 'The song she sings is easier to understand and more interesting. She is too well-bred to show her disappointment. If you ask her, her response is always well-balanced. She is old and tired, and in this instance her judgement is at fault. She is now affected with diabetes. Her eyesight too has dimmed, and so she fails to mark the signs of weakness and dissipation that were already written on her face.'

'This Old People's Home is really proud of her,' said Sadananda steadily looking at the open windows of the room

'Let her live alone. She is a talented Ghazal singer as well as being a well-groomed woman. You know religion is not only an integral part of life; it is the first, the foremost energy-consumer. All elderly persons, like all human doing, are subordinate to divine interpretation, implicit in all actions. Birth, copulation, and death are not the cycle of the anthropocentric. Our size of sorrow is proportionate to our deeds. All happenings in the Universe are but a reflection. Do you understand what I say, Sadananda?'

He only bent down his head in shame.

'How long are you waiting here for your son, grandmother?' asked Sadananda. He spoke with a palpable effort and in a voice that was barely a whisper.

Her unconcealed anger bubbled up inside her. As she was about to step back, she turned back with her short neck and said to him, 'Worthless! Not to live in her tongue and heart. The sandal tree grows not in every wood! Light is young, the ancient light; shadows are of the moment, they are born old. Shadows of my son are always suspicious and distrustful. All we want is not to get on with our life. The wise say if you seek, you will miss. Don't seek, and you will find.'

He was not able to cope with the stresses and strains of the situation. The warm, moonlit stillness around the Old People's Home was another world which had nothing in common with the turmoil and tensions and restlessness that were a part of the daylight hours.

She turned her face away and wept: wept hopelessly and helplessly and silently; the hot tears running into the grass roots as swiftly as the raindrops that had poured down on to them the day before. The rain had stopped suddenly. New grass and leaves and creepers and every variety of growing thing had sprung up overnight in lush abandoned maidan. The damp heat was less

bearable than the dry heat had been. She wept out audibly and repeatedly, and watched the shadows of nearby trees with well-founded suspicions.

Sadananda remained silent. She talked rapidly and almost inaudibly in an undertone. A tiny inner voice insisted. She looked sullen and silent, standing there on her own. The delay, to her, was a long standing dream that came true. Never before had she had a chance to peer into all the dark corners of the old age and to penetrate the mysterious, dusty darkness of loneliness in old age.

Sadananda looked up. It was past noon and great grey clouds were piling like shadowed snowdrifts against the wall of sky. The sun was bright and hot. It dazzled off the maidan and hurt his eyes. It burnt his shoulders and his arms and his face. But it didn't warm him inside. He skirted a hedge of shrubbery where the water and the earth at its base. His feet squelched and the black mud oozed coldly between his toes. He got back to the Old People's Home where all the suppressed, oppressed, and neglected old women were waiting for their nearest and dearest ones.

It was beginning to grow dark and, for the first time, she began to feel the heavy, insidious cold under her muffler. There was a brittle tension in the air, and the sharp cold pulled her nostrils together with each indrawn breath.

He listened to her quiet voice, gazing into her clear truthful eyes. A shocking rudeness was visible in her face. The past slowly drifted out of her thought. He was faced with the most question of his life. The question no doubt was innocently meant, but its answer would entail considerable explanation. Sadananda Manna crimsoned, trying hard to leave the place.

Looking at her departure, he mumbled, 'You help me build up a picture of life, my grand-mother. Working with older people, many help them relive. Man's main concern is not to gain pleasure or to avoid pain but rather to see a meaning in his life. All political leaders have exercised dictatorial control over the office with the magisterial tone of their pronouncements. All through man's history, there has been a competition between the safe and the adventurous.'

It's nearly 6 o'clock. She must get the supper. Kalpana Devi got back to her room. She shut the door behind her and leant tiredly against it, released at last from the necessity of keeping her features composed and her lips smiling. She could cry now that there was no one to see, and let tears relieve some of the strain and the pain of disappointment that the day had brought her.

But she did not cry. She looked about the high-ceilinged room with its whitewashed walls and long windows opening to a deep verandah. A room that was as utterly unlike an English bedroom as the vast, slow-moving Hooghly is unlike an English stream. The sky was a wash of clear pale green in which the first stars were already ghostly points of light, and the evening air was full of sounds; half-forgotten and yet wholly familiar sounds.

She was awakened in the diamond-bright morning by a scream from a paralysed woman, whose room gave on to the same verandah, and a moment later she herself, clad in a white cotton sari and with her soft fair curls in tangled disarray, appeared in her room.

A sturdily-built man, a Bengalee, had walked into her room, she announced in trembling tones. 'He is a physically strong and healthy man, Kalpana Devi! He didn't even knock! He just walked in! I thought I should have swooned with fright!'

'What did he want?' enquired Kalpana Devi

'Oh, he didn't want anything. He brought me tea and fruit. He just put them on a table beside my bed and went out again. Don't laugh, Kalpana Devi! It is most unkind of you! I was never so frightened in my life!'

'That was only the newly-appointed bearer,' said Kalpana Devi, continuing to laugh. 'He brought me some too. You will have to get used to it, my sister, and darling. I do not think servants in Bengal ever knock.'

'I shall never get used to it!' declared the woman, shuddering.

'Oh, yes, you will. I prophesy that within a year you will find yourself quite unable to support life or to run the simplest ménage without the assistance of at least three servants.'

Next day morning, she was laid in bed, feeling very stressed and tired. As the news got around the Old People's Home, all boarders got into the room and stood around the bed. The room was strangely quiet. Sadananda was standing close to her bed. He said to her in strict confidence, bending his head forward, 'Your son may come tomorrow, grandmother.'

She looked at him in a very weird and wonderful way and said, lying on the bed: 'Tomorrow! Tomorrow is not possible, it is always today. It is always the present that is there. The future is just in the mind, in the imagination. If my son comes, you'll not let him into my bed. Always keep it mind. Do you have ever looked at the mirror on the shelves, Sadananda?'

'Why?' asked he inquisitively

Kalpana Devi stared at him in a smiling gesture and said: 'If you look at the glasses with the light filtering through them, you'll see your face like a shadow in the mirror, between the shelves. Everybody looks glamorous and handsome in that mirror.'

'Why?' asked he again, widening the eyes

'You didn't show your skin up fine and clear, or the outlines of your face, it wasn't that kind of light. In this mirror you had dramatic shadows and sharp angles and high-lights, and you stared into your own eyes because you had never noticed them that way before, how deep and interesting they looked.' She remained silent.

A few strands of her grey hair had fallen over her forehead. For in her she cared little, having no more any love of life, but rather a desire to die.

Raising her eyes heavenward, she softly recited a poem in a half-intonation:

'I came out alone on my way to my tryst,

But who is this that follows me in the silent dark?

I move aside to avoid his presence but I escape him not.'

'This stanza has the elegance and precision. I hope you have lapped up every word of this poem. Well, of course, I want no chaos,' said she half-heartedly---only a look and a voice, then darkness again and a silence. Her words died on her lips. Her voice was getting weaker and weaker, and finally disappeared. She took a noisy gulp of tea. She often said: 'Old age is not as honourable as death, but most people want it. For death to meet us in old age is quicker and easier. If we keep our face always toward the sunshine, shadows will fall behind us. Life is not always a quest for amusement and adventure.' She was speechless for a moment, lowering her head down.

She also said: 'The British had conquered the conquerors: Maratha, Rajput and Sikh; now if the British themselves were to fall, chaos would follow. Out of that chaos might not the moon of Islam rise once more and the followers of the Prophet rule the land as they had ruled in the great days of Akbar—of Jahangir—of Shahjehan. She had always taught her juniors to be graceful in defeat.'

All remained silent, looking at her wrinkled face. There was a feeling of gloom and depression in their faces. Some boarders, dearly close to her, cried out loudly and without restraint under strong impulse of grief. Sadananda had to cry despite himself. He had been desolated by the death of Kalpana Devi. She was very impressive in appearance in her death-bed. He gave her a big sloppy kiss at her feet. He came downstairs and got astonished at the train of many bereaved age-old persons---utterly bereft of having lost a close friend--- waiting downstairs to pay their heart-felt respect to her on a noble and commanding scale. He then spoke to himself: 'It's an irreparable loss to me. She bled inwardly. All of us did a lot of irredeemable mistakes.'

Chapter II

As soon as the news of Kalpana Devi's death came to other Old People's Homes, all other ageing persons felt aggrieved, expressing their condolences with complete confidentiality. Her personality was the result of conditioning from her parents and society.

There was a lot of sun on the street; it was always such a fresh surprise to find that. Four ageing persons of Old People's Home passed a news-stand on the corner of the street, where the subway entrance dropped down, magazines draped all over it, papers heaped high on the counter. Even on them, the sun looked good, making the paper very bright and clean-looking, with the big black letters at the top: Sons celebrated mother's death anniversary in whiskey.

They stood there a moment looking down. There was a wizened, tough-looking little man inside the canopy of magazines. He poked his head out at them like a large inquisitive mole, with beady eyes that roved up and down, took them in every inch. He worked hard at a roguish smile. They left the place without a word.

Two men of Old People's Home were present at that time. One tall and turbaned, his hawk nose was clear-cut against the starlight; the other stout and muffled in a shawl that was wound about his shoulders and over his head as though to guard against the night air. The tall man did not walk furtively as the others had done. He strode past, brushing against the grasses, careless of noise, and although he spoke in an undertone his words were clearly audible.

'Dogs and devil-worshippers!' said the tall man furiously. 'Must they stoop to such filth to ensure that none shall betray them for gain? Now are all our heads forfeit for this night's work!'

'Hush---oh, hush!' begged the stout man, pausing to peer anxiously over his shoulder.

Down through the years he had never seen such a gathering of old persons as were badly affected by desertions. They sat there dumb and

inscrutable, gazing with lost eyes down the length of that great Old People's Home. Most of them had come from the uncultivated land and the dark barrier of jungle to take shelter in Old People's Homes. Thorn bushes and the tough jungle grass had thrust their way to the city. They bowed their head, folding their hands meekly on their breast. There was a feeling of gloom and depression in their faces. The open space in maidan was crowded with shadowy figures and sibilant with whispering voices.

Dead tired of age, the elderly persons of Old People's Homes didn't sleep much better in this sickly climate. Once or twice they were conscious of shouts and music. Then after what seemed a century of sleep they had heard again the drunken voice singing as it climbed the stairs to bed.

The maidan spreads for miles. None can study the map of maidan and search out the quickest route. Temples, Mosques, and Churches stand aright, looking all around with their striking beauty, pride and respect, in the glories of old Calcutta. The city awoke to a bright morning. The city had been in the grip of a cold wave for the last twelve days. As the fog was dissipated by the morning sun, the awed faces of some elderly persons were drifting away from the maidan by ones, twos and making their way through the lanes and by-lanes.

A group of morning walkers was seen walking together in an unsteady way, inclusive elderly persons, with the sun waking slowly, the birds waking noisily, school-going children appearing, splendid, rosy, cold, and awful. The office-goers went past the slum areas where the rustic women were busy in constant and boisterous brawling with neighbours from dawn-to-dusk.

Passers-by didn't need to spring upon them with attention; tourist-voracious and greedy of strangeness were all part of each other around the maidan. Looking all around, an ageing person laughed in glee and muttered: 'As dreams are more vivid than reality—perhaps because we have verbalized reality out of existence, or perhaps because our verbalizations create for us an unreal world, and below it, well below the slime of our talk, lies hidden all people do not wish to know about themselves and their world.'

Down through the ages, Calcutta has seen many political upheavals and societal changes. The city has always uttered with unrestrained outcry and grown up in an atmosphere of violence and insecurity. The tired-looking elderly persons---widows, widowers, forsaken husbands, lovers of different ages entertaining romantic thoughts, and dwellers of unpretentious old people's home--- got used to passing the winter in maidan to bask in the sun. At this ripe age, they felt a light breeze blowing over the maidan. A period of commotion and pandemonium had followed the collapse of British regime in Calcutta. This city, like forests, has its dens in which hide all their vilest and most treacherous monsters.

Calcutta maidan, as blithe and sunny as the summer days, has always been warm and blessedly familiar to all---drunkards, murderers, criminals looking awkward, snatchers and stupid, vagabonds, hawkers hawking away and deceivers deceiving away the customers all day long, call girls, trudging wayfarers, football and cricket grounds attached to the affiliated clubs of India, and political leaders shouting slogans full of beguiling voice and empty promises to achieve power ---that's the shooting script behind the bewildering maze of Calcutta maidan. Maidan has always been a nest of thieves and cattle-lifters.

The police, having been tired of patrolling the maidan at night, got back to the police station in a brisk pace in the small hours of morning to have hundreds and thousands of rupees in their pockets. A win-win smile radiated their self-confidence. They liked living in darkness, not in light. Its surroundings blend traditional and modern buildings. A herd of cattle was grazing in the vast region of maidan, together with the distant bleating of sheep, the talking of parrots, the lively buzzing of flies, the barking of stray dogs fighting with each other over a piece of bone.

Some children of broken homes and unfashionable neighbourhoods were seen playing shirtless over the pavements, unmindful of the sun's punishing rays. They were born and brought up in the underprivileged areas of the city. There were sick to their stomach. Mother was seen lulling her baby to sleep. She was looking at the touching innocence in her child's eyes.

Looking at the deplorable condition of children, an elderly man flung the contents of his glass with a violent gesture over the roses below the railings of verandah, and said bitterly: 'When a child learns to write, he learns to communicate. This is a creative beginning of a child. Since Independence children have stood alone between ever-changing conditions and never-changing principles. Tragedy is where children wail, and women weep.'

His wife, spruced herself with a lady's coat and standing off him, mumbled: 'Your words were a confirmation rather than a query.'

The city warmly greeted the rosy-coloured dawn to gather life's roses. This has been happening down the ages always. But people go on changing the history. They looked at a flock of birds, flying away as the crow flies, uttering successive chirping noises. Some tree sparrows were flying away, uttering a succession of musical tones. Calcutta is a rare mélange of the past. Looking at the good-looking but bewitching beauty of Calcutta, a septuagenarian person said in a nice gesture, 'The city-- offering a haven of peace and quietude from the bustle of the city-- never fails to enchant artist, poets, writers, filmmakers, photographers and tourists.'

'Is it so?' an elderly one, stretching out his sciatic legs on a grassy land, said in a low happy voice, 'Strange it is! It's wonderful! Honour is safe, at a ruinous cost.'

A retired Prof. Anadi Chatterjee, aged about 73, sitting behind him, suspiciously glanced at him, wondering at the inexplicable, almost rapturous expression of his clear hazel eyes and the lingering smile on his face. He knitted his brows and said:

'Oh Lord! Goodness gracious! Do you know foreign tourists regard Calcutta as a cultural icon of the city? Since the end of the 19th century hand-pulled rickshaws have been plying the streets of Calcutta. It is a British heritage in Calcutta's colonial treasure. Do you know the history of Bengal is like a river made up of the events which happen, and a violent stream; for as soon as a thing has been seen, it is carried away, and another comes in its place, and this will be carried away soon? The better-off people live in the older section of town. Love Dog one time and Dog will love you ten times. Do you understand what I say?'

He remained soundless. He bowed leaving his question unanswered. The air flowed in broad tranquil waves, lots of it, filling one's lungs with its exhilarating freshness.

Prof. Chatterjee, looking all round, said further in a low voice:

'Calcutta was once filled with panic in those days, as telegram after telegram, message after message, brought news of disaster. Delhi snatched from the hands of the British in an hour! Meerut, with one of the strongest British garrisons in India, bewildered and helpless and apparently unable to do more than protect itself from a peril that had passed from it to spread out like a forest fire over half India. With many of us, those unforgotten days seem to fall by the wayside. With the outbreak of World War II, we all..... At this age, I'm like a boat. The boat is at the bank, but there is no boatman. I haven't yet got to know the purpose of our life.'

His voice was trembling with sincerity. He heard the birds twittered but there was a kind of uncertainty in their talk.

There were some twenty dazed and terrified elderly persons, herded together, like sheep in that maidan, got astonished at the message. There had been no word from anybody else present there. All others tried to wipe from memory those gruesome scenes. They kept avoiding Ganesh Mondal, aged about 75, who used to come to maidan for a walk with his left hand paralysed. What kind of a man, in a straight-laced community, would have the courage to marry a prostitute of Sonagachi—a well-known red-light areas-- and still held his head high as some morning walkers had apparently done? They wondered what perverse psychological quirk had brought him back to the scene of repeated disasters. He was seated alone under the shadow of a tree, paralysed with fear of death.

The elderly persons felt a deep helpless sympathy for Ganesh Mondol who had lost something irreplaceable. It didn't matter what the girl had been. He had loved her who died later on. He understood now the deep resentment in his eyes, the grim mask of his face. He was a man who'd been beaten to his knees so often at the lawn of Sonagachi that he had nothing left but defiance. She wished he knew more about her. She said, 'Do you know anything about my life before you came here?'

There were only three age-old widows, and all three were just ordinary women with many of the frailties and faults common to humankind.

All began asking Prof. Chatterjee singing something so as to calm down the highly-volatile situation. The requests seemed to give him pleasure, for he flushed and brightened and turned to his wife. She was sixty-seven---a dumpy and a self-confident housewife.

'What shall I sing at this age, Leela,' said Prof. Chatterjee. His mouth was spread wide in his rare big smile. He turned to see her, in delight. He laughed in glee, because it was good to get a response from his wife.

'Sing something touching,' the old lady said, 'something that grips the heart.'

'Sing that new song of yours,' his wife said, 'you sing better than I do. Some things are better left unsaid.' She turned off her head. She saw that the bungalow had laid tree-lapped in drowsiness and heat. There was no one. Even the grass was straight; one could not make out the imprint of those evil sinful bodies who had sat on it in the morning.

His wife's expressive dark eyes tilted slightly upwards at the outer corners, which women pronounced unbecoming and men found irresistible. An uprush of gaiety and high spirits and an irrational desire ran out into the sunlight and shout and play foolish games. To laugh for the sheer joy of laughing and to make up for all the laughter had been lost during the lonely years in Old People's Home.

'Eh? Oh sure, sure,' said Prof. Chatterjee, turning round. He was happy, telling stories of his early days. He listened, laughed at the right places. So did his wife.

'What do you think, my darling?' asked his wife in a silky voice free of dissimulation.

Looking at the grey-coloured sky, Prof. Chatterjee said in a grave voice: 'We are all misunderstood. Our sons were unable to understand the treasures rested up in our heart---treasures of charity, piety, temperance and soberness. They assailed us with stinging words. These treasures we take with us beyond death when we will leave the world.'

'Don't dwell on the past. What's past is past. All are selfish. Twisting is one of the deep-rooted things in them—diplomacy, politics, and cunningness,' said his wife, 'you now sing a song.'

Prof. Chatterjee slipped the walking stick off his hand. A walking stick was a last resort to a man of old age. He took his seat by his wife, looking forward to bettering his acquaintance with the new members. He raised his face and began singing in a slightly husky but strong and stirring voice. The World War II was narrated in that brief prelude. The elderly persons sat listening with an air of expectancy.

'Don't cry for me, my little wife,

I lost my blood, 'tis true,

But gladly would I give my life

To save my land and you'

His eyes were half-shut and his head ceased twitching. The menace of the past sounded ever more strongly through the flood of joyous moment. It was inseparable. It hovered around the maidan; it sped down the crowded car running past the maidan, incarnate in this man and the song he was singing. He

sang the couplet and fell silent. His hand round her wrist did not hurt her in presence of others.

All sat without stirring. They were silent, in the grip of a common thought, a single emotion, that of elderly persons sharing the same destiny, elderly persons who had passed through the fire of ordeal with honour. They all had the same thoughts as welded them together more strongly than iron.

An old woman, sitting close to Leela, cried softly, and Leela made no attempt to wipe her own wet eyes. A few minutes later, Prof. Chatterjee and his wife left the place without a word.

Suddenly, they heard 'La Ill-ah ha! Ill-ah ho!' cried the muezzins from the minarets of the mosques in the city. 'There is no God but God!' They listened to the sounds of prayer fade and die. Nothing seemed to stir in that cold, breathless stillness; no twig or leaf or dry spear of grass. There seemed to be nothing alive in maidan except home-bound workers and running vehicles.

The elderly persons felt sun-drenched drowsiness after lunch. Loveliness; the discovery was confirmed after the British Raj had left India, of the promised land, the flesh in beauty, swinging with it in unison the spirit; a great hurt in the breast, and all the words that this pain had created through the ages came true; the lovely words, more rousing, more important than cares of hands or contact of flesh in the sumptuous creation and maintaining of desire.

At this advanced age, they were as unsteady as a shadow in their movement. Most of them were unattractive in appearance. Those culturally homogeneous neighbourhood persons were ostracized, neglected, and overlooked and seen no longer as bearers of wisdom but as embodiment of shame and humiliation. They could feel their legs tottering and their voice faltering. Therefore, some of them had to come to maidan by hand-pulled rickshaws. Calcutta's legacy of hand-pulled rickshaws dates back to Shimla, which was the summer capital for the officials of the East India Co.

At this seasoned age, they suffered multi-morbidity---prolonged sickness, dependence, pain, and suffering. Even they didn't like any threateningly sudden

or deceptive moves. And they got to know careless talk costs loves. A false sense of security was hanging over them. The sunlight sparkled like jewellery all over the maidan, hitting the lush green field in winter.

They---a familiar association of old friends--- lived alone in old people's homes lying outside maidan. The old people's homes satisfied themselves with rooms, furniture, books and clothes that were worn and homely and friendly to the touch. Home is where the heart is. They felt completely at home living in a comfortable position with respect to some objective. Most of them got tired of indefatigable struggle for existence and strongly motivated striving with million-fold multiplied means of problems of life in Calcutta.

They were conscious of a twinge of anxiety as to what the sudden summons might portend. They could think of nothing that had not already received their attention. An unutterable sadness was looming large over their faces. They felt so near to one another as if nothing could draw them nearer.

Only ominous clouds of loneliness were gathering round them. They got to feel times were different in their old age. Everything was getting pretty old now. They discerned a strange odour coming out from stale food. Most of the criticisms were made on the habits of the poor by the well-housed, well-warmed, and well-fed.

An indescribable sound rose from the crowd; a sound like the soft growling snarl of a gigantic cat, all of them rose on their walking-sticks and facing the house which was on fire. They could feel the pulse and panic of the city swirling about the dwellers from the very dust and beating down upon the pedestrians in the binding heat. The air was hideous with sound---the strange swishing roar of the flames, the cracking of fire-expanded bricks, the falling of masonry, the shouts and curses of men, the changing of bells as other fire trucks raced towards other fires, running footsteps, the gushing of water from hoses, car horns, breaking glass, screams for help, weeping, moaning….

At length the noise died down. Suddenly, they found a house was on fire farther up the street. Flames were surging from the upper windows like the tongues of some multi-headed monster. People were running towards it, calling to each other. 'There's someone in the bedroom! Ladders—fetch ladders! Call the firemen!' Other colleagues guided his footsteps towards the incident.

A handsome young man, together with other several persons, standing anxiously from a distance, had sought after their beloved ones for long. The young man was threading his way towards the burning spot between the exclaiming, arguing groups. They didn't know whether their beloved ones were alive or not.

The roofs of the houses had caved in; the fire began to die a little in the first house and was brought under control next door. The roofs of the houses had caved in. The crowd drew forward to look. The firemen tried holding them back. 'Now then, now then---there's bodies in there. We've got to get them out. Clear the way, please, clear the way...'

They looked all around the maidan. Leaves were silent around flowers which were their words. Beauty smiled in the confinement of the bud, in the heart of a sweet incompleteness. The city offered a singularly fascinating mix of old architects of British Raj and new palatial buildings.

Like all other elderly persons, Mr. Shibnath Mitra woke very late the following morning. He had gone to bed with little more said, but he had turned and tossed for endless in the darkness, sleepless and alone. He knew himself lost and without guidance as all other elderly persons, looking at the statue that was once deemed the acme of beauty.

Dawn was late on that misty December morning in Calcutta, and he just remembered hearing the birds crying and seeing a greyness encroach upon the bar of night between the curtains; he was about to get and pull the curtains when he fell asleep. And all other boarders of old people's home were still lying in bed.

Mr. Shibnath Mitra had pulled back the curtains and the window let in a shaft of wintry sun. He was six feet tall and thin with grey hair. Red-eyed and collarless, he smiled unconvincingly at the boy. The mouth was trying to turn up but the lines turned down. He looked out the window, remembering the days of his first romance with Sanjukta das: 'Her little lips were forming the words as she went from line to line. She was wearing the same dress as she wore every night and he suspected it was not off; it's stiff lace collar and heavily brocaded front with flaps and frills over it looked out of place this morning. She didn't even take off her earrings or the four strings of pearls.'

It was Sunday. To all retired persons, everyday was a holiday, resting away from home. The elderly persons, looking at the vast stretch of field, were holidaying in a pleasant sunlight in maidan. An unfathomable weight of sleep pressed them down every day. Hundreds and hundreds of young boys were playing soccer in the sun all day. A sciatic elderly one was spitting his words scornfully against the chaotic situation around them. The sun was shining like a goldsmith's shop in Cheapside. The sight of the maidan was as charming as inspiring to them.

A well-meaning elderly man was—Mr. Shibnath Mitra at 70—seen standing on crutches on the narrow pavement of Esplanade-- steadily looking at the signal when the running vehicles would come to a stop. He was waiting there for a little while. As the signal was red, he gave a cry of relief. He crossed the road with stupendous effort to reach the maidan, leaning on two long wooden crutches. He roused himself from his stupor of cold and fatigue and peered ahead. The roads around maidan were lined with shade trees, grey with the dust of breathless but panting days and the sharp-edged shadows of any one of them might have swallowed up the figure of that lame man getting forward to maidan. His movement stretched away to the left and right past the vehicles.

For a time his strength of body and natural health stood him in good stead, but eventually indulgence and dissipation began to take their toll, aided as they were by climate, the conditions of life in Calcutta, and the growing old age.

On the way to maidan, Mr. Mitra muttered, looking at helpless parents squatting on a dust-ridden pavement beset with cow-dung: 'What a fool I had

been! What an unutterable fool to take chances when such a dazzling future was at stake! In the present century, the problem is that the elderly persons are neglected. Our sons are false friends, unjust judges, hypocrites, sincere in hatred, jealous, vain and revengeful, false in promises, honest in curse, suspicious and hideous to their elderly parents. I wonder what has become of him. When faith is lost, honour dies. I do not know what I shall find in their old age.'

Mr. Mitra's recollections of old days were hazy. His head hurt abominably, his jaw ached, and his parched mouth was full of blood from a cut that his teeth had made in his tongue. He got to feel: 'How long have I been in Old People's Home? Three months? Or is it four? It feels like years to me. All old persons are in the same boat.' He closed his eyes and leant his aching head against a tree.

He suddenly heard a short-lived commotion about a squatter sitting near a restaurant. He squared his shoulders and got to know that a tender-aged boy had kicked out the elderly person from the doorways and battered that emaciated person until he fell down. None had come to rescue him. He left the place, lying down to go to sleep somewhere others didn't normally sleep.

There was a rustle in the grasses and a voice whose owner remained invisible spoke in a whisper that was barely audible above the creaking of a distant running vehicles. Putting under his arms two long wooden crutches, Mr. Mitra looked at the blue sky. The cry of some crows was seen circling overhead a tree. Some gaily coloured kites flew all day and at all seasons in the sky above the city, and a strayed one that had broken its string was frequently to be found tangled among the branches of trees on the plain.

There was a red kite caught in the thorn tree by the city road. Another cheap paper kite was caught up in its scanty spiked foliage. Mr. Mitra didn't pass the thorn trees and barely glanced at them. He took a narrow side-path to reach the maidan--- a place of trillion mosquitoes. He took a deep breath, ducked his head under and then flung himself forward with his walking stick, arms flailing wildly. His whole body was numb with the icy pain of his leg

amputated. He took another deep breath. When he put his face down, the cold made his temples ache. The cold became a tingling delight.

Mr. Mitra, slinging his torn bag over his shoulder, arrived at the maidan where his fellow-friends were eagerly waiting for him, staring at the oldest road on the maidan, extending from 'Cocked hat' in the north to the Khidderpore Bridge.

Mr. Mitra stretched out his hand and took the small flat cake of coarse-ground floor, and stood looking down at it with the smile that he had taught himself to wear when his face was being watched by tense or frightened men for a clue to his thoughts. Mr. Mitra had to move aside for a blind old man, who had been tapping along behind him and now came up closer. He was staring ahead into his very black lenses intently as blind men do, his chin thrust forward and his whole body pointed ahead in watchfulness, as he hammered hard and rhythmically at the pavement with his heavy stick. He had an old man's face, eyeless behind the daylight, gray and disconsolate and truculent, t said: 'don't tread on me, why me? I didn't, but we are all.' The stick was held at the crook, and it lifted up and down in short arcs, and the steel end struck with force.

That blind old man, clothed with worn garments, appeared there singing a traditional song. Early in the morning, just as the sun was rising, he heard an old man sing in severe depression. Mr. Mitra heard this song after a lapse of several years like all those who had lapsed their valuable times in a chatty talk. He smiled, as though solaced by the memory. The old man then sang with full voice, pure and clear, uplifted, as some classic melody in sweetest legends of old minstrelsy:

'God be in my eyes,

And in my looking

God be in my mouth,

And in my speaking;

God be in my heart,

And in my thinking;

God be at my end, And at my departing'

Mr. Mitra turned off his face to the west and laughed aloud in sheer delight. Looking all around, he saw several elderly men and women, from different directions, were getting to maidan, like the leisurely gait of summer, to bask in the sun. He stood there with his crutches. Looking at the sequence of their foot movements, he mumbled 'Old age is not as honourable as death, but most people want it. I would like to be buried with great pomp and somberness. We are dying; we are dying, and then--nothingness! So it is better to be a has-been than a never-was. But there were no more days--only hours. We can't…' He didn't complete the sentence but looked past.

He further stutteringly stepped forward to maidan, feeling under the weather. The muffler sat beautifully around his neck. Over his body was with a soft Kashmiri shawl. The 'broad graveled walk' on the west side of the portion is the Red Road, constructed in 1820. The school children were playing together not far from them. Between the silent old men and the small children there sprang up a strong bond of sympathy and understanding. They got to realize what the children must be suffering in homesickness, and they sensed the loneliness and needed for affection that lay behind the old men's forbidding exterior and irascible manner.

As Mr. Mitra appeared there, all elderly persons got pleased at his arrival. 'Why are you so late, Mr. Mitra?' asked Mr. Anil Gupta, at 67, 'You're to be serious at this age!'

'What do you mean?' Mr. Mitra's voice had a sharp edge to it.

'Sorry! It's my mistake. At this age, we all make mistake, Mr. Mitra. Do you know Calcutta is the noisiest city in South Asian cities? Unwanted and unnecessary noise---honking, loudspeakers and generator sets--- has mental and physical health repercussion. Noise is a silent killer as it affects the nervous system of old persons. So I cannot go out of the Old People's Home.' He bawled him out for being late.

Mr. Mitra raised his eyebrows and observed Mr. Gupta coldly that Mr. Gupta was mistaken in supposing that he had no knowledge of the situation. Mr. Mitra heaved a resigned sigh. Mr. Mitra murmured a few words of conventional greeting and looked beyond him into the wide. He looked long and deliberately, studying that young and guarded face; noting the weariness and schooled immobility with cool interest. He made a small swift gesture with the clenched hand.

They all were burst into gales of laughter. The noise coming out from the political procession made him sweat, and little prickling of nervousness ran out to his finger-tips like pins and needles.

Two of his fellow-friends quickly rose to their feet and helped him take his seat on a green grass. Holding the crutch carefully and watchfully, he took his seat. He put down his glasses, wiping out his dust-ridden eyes with the handkerchief. The procession of a misleading political party, hankering after power and money, was walking down the broad way of Esplanade with high-pitched slogans—the single biggest contributor to noise pollution in Calcutta. In the procession was there a hidden network of criminals. There was a stir and babble among the crowd. Ill-temper, enmity, malice, had flourished unawares in the midst of procession.

'No,' said Mr. Mitra evenly, leaving a sigh of relief and looking at the procession, 'none of us finds life supportable at this age. Day after day, countless people die. Yet people live as though they are never going to die. Can you tell me why there are no difference between man and swine? Can you tell me why today and tomorrow will be yesterday?'

'Why do you say so, Mr. Mitra?' asked another one, sitting close to him, with inquiring mind. A salvo of questions confused him.

Mr. Mitra was laughing too loud looking sideways at some others napping leaning back against the old trees. Looking at him with rapt attention, Mr. Mitra said in a dignified and stately tone, 'The future never comes in. Tomorrow is not possible. It is always today. It is always the present that is there. The future is just in the mind, in the imagination. It is a dream; it is not a part of reality. Happiness in today's world has become elusive.' Mr. Mitra became broodingly morose.

'We can't understand what you say, Mr. Mitra. Please, clarify it,' said one of his colleagues. He kept saying aloud, 'Oh, oh, oh!'

'We live ignorant and die in errant as we lived in overcrowded conditions. Many of us would be nowhere else if given the choice. But as a general rule these fall into two categories: those who remain, and endure every hardship that heat and disease and exile can bring, for love of husband or father. And those whose social status in this country is such that India gives them a sense of position and importance that they cannot obtain here. The rest hate it. We do nothing in the world but lie. You know a good person is like a sandal tree and the world is like a snake. The snake resides on the tree but the sandal tree doesn't become poisonous to any extent. The poor have no friends. May God give you good morrow! '

All of his elderly colleagues felt embarrassed that they had been so lucky to meet him. They watched him carefully with interest.

All remained quiet in the midst of political slogans creating an unpleasant and hostile situation by uninvited and undesirable verbal and physical conduct. The city was in a shambles after independence. Mr. Mitra had arrived in a singularly unpleasant frame of mind.

One of his colleagues stared at him, his eyes hot with a hopeless anger that was as much against himself as Mr. Shibnath Mitra, and he said violently and as though the words were wrenched from him: 'Yes---God damn self-centered political parties for their aggressive selfishness! Everyone has been frightened by the strange sequence of events. They have been afflicted either with moral and political bankruptcy. When we are getting young, we can see for miles from here. As we are getting old, we can't see to read. At this age, we don't seek for path, but path seeks after us. Thoughts of domestic violence on

property bring destruction to all harmony, well-being, restfulness and content. I think it so.'

Mr. Kashinath Dutta felt his insides quivering and a tiny film of cold sweat began to bead his forehead. He bit his lower and put his head down. After a moment he felt a little less dizzy. He then raised his face.

Mr. Kashinath Dutta looked at him approvingly and smiled, and said: 'Thank you for being with us. I know. The only argument you understand. But today I didn't come here to quarrel.' As always, he said little and picked up his Kashmiri shawl and slowly began to brush it with his long fingers, for the entire world.

'Don't be excited, Kashinath!' said Mr. Mitra gravely, 'Last month you felt chest pains—a warning signal of your heart problems.' Mr. Mitra was conscious of a cold tingling sensation between his shoulder-blades and was aware that his mouth was dry.

'Hmm,' said Mr. Kashinath Dutta biting his lips nervously, 'yes, you're right. You have touched a raw nerve when you mention my chest pains.'

Looking at him, Mr. Dutta said with respect: 'the cultural life of the country has sunk into shrivel unless more artists and writers emerge. Our political leaders have possessed a love of two things that have never yet failed to ruin those devotees who have worshipped them to excess: Drink and Women. Everyone can show the way to a blind man, nobody can show the way to a stupid person as our political leaders do. I think I die tonight! Am I right Mr. Mitra? Is there any mistake?' Nightmare-like now, he was gripped with an urgent necessity to know the worst.

Mr. Shibnath Mitra digested this statement in silence. He had had barely three hours' sleep in the last two days and his head was aching. His amputated leg was absurdly painful and it throbbed to a steady burning beat of pain while walking on the way. Raising his eyes heavenward, he grimly muttered: 'Goodness gracious! Her father didn't have to have his other leg amputated. Had her father broken my other leg, what would have happened to my lot? The

rich gallery of characters in this city has always cursed at the vast society of have-nots. Thank goodness that's over!'

Mr. Shibnath Mitra looked very strong and hard, his eyes were somehow stark and motionless, his smile lay on the surface, proceeding from nowhere, his voice was clipped, hearty tenors.

Evening was looming large over the city by slow degrees. The local street-dogs that used to roaming about the maidan were observing them with their steady eyes. Mr. Mitra gave a slight shrug of his shoulders and said nothing further.

As he looked forward to the maidan, an old and weary beggar was seen going past the passers-by, singing a traditional folk song:

'I long to live in utter loneliness,

With none to speak to, none to share my thoughts'

The voice ceased, and there was silence. But now there was blankness about them and they seemed to look at each other. Mr. Mitra had heard Beggar's footsteps and his quiet voice. Then his lips and eyes were touched and sealed with silence and darkness, so that he was dumb and blind. Then through the silence came a sound like the booming of the sea. He saw the bright, transient colour flood up into Mr. Dutta's pale face and his eyes mislaid their blankness and became brilliant again. Mr. Mitra was absorbed in deep thought.

Leaning on the scrawny crutch, the strength within him began to fail. He felt his life ebbing at its springs. Death seemed to draw near to him and his shape was Silence. He entered at his heart, entered with a sense of numbing cold, but his brain was still alive, he could yet think. He knew that he was drawing near the confines of the Dead. He heard a tuneful music blared from the open window of the house across the way. He got his own way in the end, when someone tried to stop him.

'What are you thinking, my friend?' asked Mr. Dutta, raising his eyebrows and staring at his gloomy face overcast with depressing outline of darkness. Mr.

Mitra paused significantly before he answered. Having seen some call girls sauntering about the maidan to catch the home-going customers, Mr. Mitra felt shocked.

'Not at all,' said Mr. Mitra looking at him fondly with a smiling gesture, 'A wife's place is with her husband---unless he should be brutal or diseased or insane. The marriage ceremony was entered into freely---I might even say eagerly. There's no legal reason why I should be summarily deserted. Mind is nothing but thoughts. The purpose of our old persons is to have a happy life. Intolerance today makes the Indian society dirty, strained, and discoloured. To me, life is 10% to indulge in dreaming away hours, and 90% to face the harsh reality. Do you know ideas create stupidity because the more the ideas are there, the more the mind is burdened?' He was smiling, but his eyes retained a look of solemnity.

Saying so, he looked at the other man pointedly. There was a flicker in his eyes. He turned sharply away with a gesture of impatience. As the evening was approaching, they knew, the aggressive breakup of organized criminal gangs would begin dancing over the maidan. It was very hard for them to work in the day---specially, when it was so warm and sunny outside.

All got to know that an unprecedented misfortune had happened to him in his young age. He was like Jerusalem's temple, interior all light, but outside the walls are in ruinous plight. He had fought a perpetual battle with the daily problem of how to do what appeared to him as obviously right, sensible and just, and at the same time steer clear of a direct collision with some senior officials who resented his early promotion and his impatience with bumbling ineptitude. He had learned a good lesson as he had come across with Sanjukta Das, aged about 22, at Science College, Rajabazar, in Calcutta. He pondered over the events of those oppressively and unpleasantly dull days of his life. It was a behind-the-scenes of his romance.

She was tall and slender and walked with a grace which was curiously interrupted at intervals by a sudden lifting upon the toes like a barely suppressed skip. She was very pretty, with curly chestnut hair swept up from the ears, large expressive black eyes and the complexion of an early peach. She was the very embodiment of the Victorian ideal of Beauty, but she didn't seem to have possessed of those beauties. She talked vivaciously to him at Science College---treating him as an equal---and bent her head in acknowledgment of a greeting from some passing friends.

Mr. Mitra stood alone looking back at some deserted wives sitting together on a bench. They were like snow and black shadows: cool and mysterious and yet---. They looked desperately unhappy and lonely. As the maidan was getting silent and deserted, he suddenly heard a sweet and placid voice of a female from behind him. Relying on his walking stick, he stood back, looking steadily at the pretty woman standing before him. He went on a few paces and stopped again. She touched at his feet to get his blessing. Looking at her, Mr. Mitra couldn't recognize her. He was strangely silent.

'Do you not recognise me, sir?' asked she in a silky tone. Mr. Mitra's face was dark against the moon and the night sky. He could see the gleam of her teeth and the glitter of her eyes, and though his first momentary panic had died at sight of her, an odd flicker of fear went through him.

He stood quite still, looking at her and rolling his eyes by way of an answer, and no longer seeing her as a forlorn child, but as an age-old woman. The small heart-shaped face was unusually pale, and the shadows under the great dark eyes made them appear even larger. The crumpled whiteness of her sari and corset cover served to turn her bare arms to a warm shade of ivory, and the loosened hair that tumbled about her in rippling profusion glinted with fluorescent lights in the cold greyness of trees.

'No. I don't,' said Mr. Mitra looking only at her with vacant eyes. Was it his fault or not? He couldn't remember her name. He finally kept an image of her face in his memory, looking at the window where the shades were down and the gauze curtains drawn over them. He touched his ear with a questioning finger. He wouldn't allow emotions to get in the way of his remembering her.

'I'm Arundhuti—Arundhuti Mukherjee. Once I was your student. You helped me solve the critical problems of physics. Do you remember as I went to your house to learn physics on every Saturday?' A dimple broke the smooth curve of her grave cheek and she smiled. The sound of the swift familiar voice revived memories of his old days.

She then knelt over her pet dog and fondled it with the tenderest stroking caresses, over its nose, along its sides, under the belly, and it arched its head back and tensed its body in sensuous delight. 'Oh-h-h, does my little Princess like to be petted? Does she like to be touched and petted? Does she like her mamma to pay attention to her?' stroking and fondling, her head bent in immolation over the shaggy little dog.

The long morning wore away, and the appalling heat filled every corner and crevice of Old People's Home as though it had been a tangible thing; a weight which could be lifted from the shoulders if only the body had possessed sufficient strength.

'You're Arundhuti! Now I recognise you. I couldn't recognise you as soon as you appeared before me. Many years have passed since we last met. It's a long time,' said he, feeling a cold southerly breeze as the cold weather was coming from the south.

'Thank Heaven! Nothing is wrong with your memory, sir,' said she in a rich and lively gesture, fondling and stroking her pet dog. Mr. Mitra then muttered in discontent: 'Good heavens! A pet dog is preferable to an age-old teacher.

'Why are you here, Arundhuti?' asked he in a careful and sensible way.

'You know everything, sir,' said she looking at him in a gloomy face, 'A day after my marriage, my husband, Mr. Agnidev Mukherjee, Flight Lieutenant, went right to the front at the call of his Air Commanding Officer as the Indo-Pak war was going on. Three-days later....' She cried noisily and uncontrollably, taking sudden, sharp breaths, expressing her sorrow at the news of her newly-married husband's death. He came close to her in a steady step, holding his walking stick with a steady hand. He stood one step ahead of her and consoled her, patting her on the back consolingly. He held his breath and slid his left hand to her shoulder.

'Why do you feel sorrowed over his death? You should be proud of our national hero. We're proud of your husband's heroic death,' said he looking at her sorrowful eyes, 'I feel sorry for yourself. None can remember us, but your husband's heroic deeds will always be everlasting to our national history. He secured a victory in the face of overwhelming odds. Life seems easy for one who is shameless, who is a crowning hero. There is nothing like a brisk walk on a cold day! Keep a green tree in your heart and perhaps a singing will come. Try to forget that, Arundhuti.'

She had the oddest feeling that her teacher was avoiding her. His advice made her live alive. Looking at her teacher's face, she said in an indistinct voice, 'A woman's heart is just like a lithographer's stone, ---what is once written upon it cannot be rubbed out. He left me alone smiling. Can you tell me how I can forget him, sir?' She wept bitter tears of distress. She put Princess down at her feet and the do stayed there, resting against her legs. 'You see,' she cried. 'She likes you; she's making friends with you already.' She leaned over to place her hand upon the shaggy head, but it turned under her and suddenly the little mouth was at her fingers, licking with startling eagerness, the tongue flashing in and out, flap-flap, liquid sound.

He hung his head in disgrace and felt that he had lost honour and respect to her. Raising his head, he kept a sharp lookout for any weirdness in life.

'Where do you live in, Arundhuti?' asked he, standing close to his student.

She flashed a pleasant smile; the smile an actress might have employed to indicate pleasurable surprise. Arundhuti said gaily and on the same note of surprise that was in her smile. The disease had reduced her to a skeleton.

'At that Old People's Home standing behind that Bank,' said she, pointing out her finger at the Bank and feeling extremely upset, 'I live there. It's only for widows to be protected from the more unpleasant difficulties of life as the people desperately seek shelter from the din and bustle of city's life. I have no sons and daughters. His death has dramatically changed my life. I'm alone today.'

Mr. Mitra stared at her with a thin face and sharp features. Her self-confidence had been completely flattened. Realising that her experience of life had shattered her illusions about love, he came close to her. She knew little or nothing of India, and the little she knew had taught her to believe that some Indians were treacherous murderers, not one of whom was trusted.

'Always remember, a perfect tragedy is the noblest production of human nature. Don't worry, Arundhuti,' said he in a gay challenging tone, 'I'm always with you. The proximity of death and its stifling closeness make me feel sick.' She thought about a situation, as if she was not involved in it herself.

She was a lonely woman, driven in upon her by the circumstances of this new life; her only companions the silent Indian women and the old women crippled by years and gout. It was not surprising that her memory painted India as a place of wonder and beauty where the sun always shone and where people didn't live in vast, chilly rooms full of ugly dark furniture, but in gardens full of strange and beautiful flowers and tame birds. A dark flight of fruit bats flapped silently across the garden of Governor's House.

Arundhuti moaned with relief as the strain was transferred to her body. Gasping and straining, he tightened his walking stick with a firm grip and stepped up as gently as he could. Tears forced themselves out of her tight shut eyes. He got to feel that she was helplessly afraid with a fear that she had never known before. A primitive, a primeval fear; not of death, but of Evil....

In the year that had followed her husband's death Arundhuti had grown paler and thinner and more silent than ever. Her skin appeared to be stretched tightly over the fine bones of her skull, making her mouth seem even wider and her eyes far too large for her small sallow face. The cruel void left by her husband's death remained unfulfilled, the natural health and resilience of youth eventually reasserted itself and a change came over. Almost overnight, or so it seemed, she grew from a plain child into a young woman of strange and disturbing beauty. Between the old teacher and the silent, dry-eyed widow there sprang a strong bond of sympathy and understanding. He saw her worst fears realized and got to the road. He walked lightly like a man in a dream.

Looking at the Governor's House, Mr. Mitra saw myriad fire-flies, in the gathering dusk, spangled the bamboo brakes with glinting pin-points of light. The evening air was full of sounds---conches blaring all around the temples, the barking of pariah dogs and all the noises of a city. He was then immersed in deep thought. Life had been almost too perfect. The good fortune which had surrounded them since their first meeting had showed no sign of lapsing. Arundhuti's speech had not surprised him, he had anticipated opposition in that quarter, but her harsh words had struck him rather painfully.

Mr. Mitra had spoken a few stiffly formal words of thanks when he had said goodbye to his student. He was astounded and disturbed to find that the sound brought him a sudden feeling of being alone and unprotected.

The hard dry ground of the mango tope did not hold the print of footmarks well, but the day was windless, and dust, twigs and fallen leaves betrayed a well-worn track from the maidan to their Old People's Home, while beyond it the print of unshod feet of age-old morning walkers showed where a single man had approached from the direction of the grazing grounds and the open plain, and returned again.

The memory of his dire misfortune cast a blank shadow over his mind for some moments. Even yet he couldn't accustom his mind to the change. He still felt that his mother existed in this world that she had gone away for many years and would soon be back; already his mind was stored up with things he wanted to say to her, little questions he wished to ask, matters which cropped up since her going and which seemed to need her personal attention. He crumpled up all of his son's letters without even looking up at it. The muscles of his face tightened up in anger.

Arundhuti stood watching him for a moment or two, and then she had gone to him and put her arms about him, and laid her cheek against his hair. He turned his head against her shoulder with a tired sigh and his arms went round her quite gently. He turned his head and looked at the set white face beside him and said after a moment: 'oh, my goodness! I feel good for you out of the goodness of my heart. I must cooperate with you till my death. My old age leads to dangerous tensions and conflict and demise at the longest.' His voice grated on her nerves, looking at the Old People's Home---the home of the unblessed. Looking at the god-awful weather, he got back to his unpleasant and disagreeable room of Old People's Home. She became broodingly morose when her teacher left her. She turned back and looked at his movement quickly and easily.

'Good night. See you in the morning, sir,' said Arundhuti, waving her nimble fingers. He remembered her pure ascetic face; it had seemed to him then the most beautiful face he knew.

'Thank you, Arundhuti,' said Mr. Mitra in a gay mood. He muttered: 'I have suffered from a series of undying feeling of pain and of worry. Scientists say that out of a hundred things, you listen to only two percent. And out of a hundred things, you see only two percent. To live two percent is almost not to live at all. What kind of life is this? We die separately and alone. Who knows my old age will end tonight?'

The dust and the acrid smoke of the dung fire penetrated through his nostrils maddeningly, and the wound in his leg troubled painfully. A procession of mosquitoes crawled across his legs and myriad night-flying insects that had been attracted by the dim glow of the fire fluttered and crept about his face.

He felt mature and lonely. The pupils of his eyes had narrowed like a cat's in the light, and he said in his soft voice whose faintly sing-song intonation alone betrayed the fact. Nothing would ever be the same. It happened—whether by accident or designs of God---that all of my friends were alone after Sanjukta, queen of his first romance, had gone leaving him alone in this deserted city of loneliness. He lowered his aching leg over the side of the bed and stood up with difficulty.

Arundhuti Devi had stood pressed against the old banyan tree and listened to the sound of his quick light steps with his walking stick dying out on the dusty road outside, and presently the night had swallowed up the sound. She looked tired and strained and that there were shadows under her eyes. But perhaps the blazing suns of the last twenty years in Delhi had thinned her blood.

To distract her thoughts from her physical discomforts she turned to the current-irritant of her present mission in Calcutta, and for perhaps the hundredth time, and with a deepening sense of exasperation and distaste, mentally reviewed the events that had led her husband towards the Great House of Death. She finally took a last refuge in Old People's Home in Calcutta to leave her last breath. The afternoon was filled with sound and sunshine. Tears of outraged vanity blurred her vision. A melancholy monotone beat on her heart. She could hear, intermittently, a murmur of voices from the upper chamber of the building behind her, but it came at longer and longer intervals and at last there was silence.

There were clouds in the sky that night, but they had no promise of rain; only of hot winds and dust, and it seemed as though they intensified the heat, pressing it down on to the gasping earth so that it could not escape, as though they were a lid on gigantic cauldron.

She stood at the bed side, all free of bonds, her hands beside her, fingers spread upon her thighs, and she echoed low, 'why don't do right—' and blind she threw her body against and impact stunned all mind.

Chapter: III

As the sun was about to sink down below the western horizon, Mr. Shibnath Mitra and other elderly persons got ready to get back to the old people's homes, uttering a wordless cry of despair. An expected sight met his eyes as he kept quickening his pace drawing near to They turned to a dead body of an age-old person lying on a dust-ridden pavement like the remains of dead animals scattered hither and thither. Mr. Mitra glared at the dead body with eyes flashing angry reproach and all others looked with a feeling of anxiety and stress. Mr. Mitra said with oath like solemnity:

'With high hope, I came to Calcutta where people do not trust each other and feel unfriendly towards each other. But all of my hopes have shattered into pieces. We all live in the protection of certain cowardices which we call our principles. Leaders first learn the meaning of what they say, and then speak. At this age, we, all fools, dwelling in darkness, go round and round, by various tortuous paths of nightmarish living conditions. Selfishness has a gloss of humanitarianism about us.'

'Good talk that!' Arundhuti's exclamation sounded low but distinct. She then sang with a lively, supple voice that Mr. Mitra had liked in college days.

He and all others got back to their own destination. He peered ahead with watering eyes, his eyelids frozen and sticky. All around was inky darkness due to power-cut. Something glimmered faintly ahead through the deep murk.

Mr. Mitra, through his sleep, heard the rain pattering steadily on the roof. The road, at midnight, murmured restlessly. The raindrops trickled slantwise down the panes. The dark sodden houses stood hunched outside the window, everything was puckered up and the rain dimpled the surface of a big puddle. He lifted his hand to knock, but his heart began pounding so violently that he could hardly catch his breath. He called the house servants.

No one answered. They had all gone out. They had let them sleep on because some boarders had come to Old People's Home late the night before. Mr. Mitra's back ached. He had been in the saddle all day long.

With every night, the boarders became ever more depressed. They were becoming increasingly sad about the way things were going on. Mr. Mitra was left alone after all the others had gone. It was getting darker and darker all over the maidan. As he went back the way he had come, he heard the chirping of crickets began making a loud high sound by rubbing their wings together. Mice were seen scampering around the big trees with short light steps to find food. A big mouse ran away, squeaking with panic. He moved a step closer to the main road. The Old People's Home, situated in a quiet spot, was only a short step from the maidan. He was stumbling across the wide maidan.

Amidst the sounds and movements of animals, call-girls, pick-pockets, snatchers, kidnappers, underworld criminals, human traffickers, and other anti-social elements got into the maidan. Mr. Mitra knew them well. He caught them up and fell into a major step beside them. Sanjukta's father had hired out some Muslim criminals from the maidan to beat him. He had been lying unconscious near a hidden area littered with household rubbish for an hour in the midst of some stray dogs and scampering rats.

After an hour, he had been hospitalized to a nearby hospital where his well-muscled leg had been amputated. The physicians had carefully examined his leg and got to feel that he was likely to have had that, and providentially he had survived to live up with dignity even with many hardships and been weighted down with cares.

He bent his knees several times to relax the muscles. He opened his eyes. Looking at the bright moonlit night, he said suddenly and loudly because of emotion:

'Oh! Good Heavens! As good luck would have been, I'm still battling on with sublime confidence to get alive with one leg. It's the gift of my first romance. As an old person, I'm not subjected to any person's sympathy. I'm like musty old books. Most of our neglected and unwanted age-old persons stay at home all-day long but I don't do so. The remainder roams about like stray dogs. None comes to feed the remains of his food to the stray dogs,' said Mr. Mitra slowly. Merely to look, what other pleasures had ever been so entirely renewing, all refugees and evacuees, after partition of India, had grown and expanded in the city of Calcutta as a grateful plant in the sun and rain.

'Thank God' thought Mr. Mitra with sudden vehemence, 'all powers in Heaven, as well as on earth, are given to the rich. It is! I'm not fated to live together with Mrs. Sanjukta Das---such is life---but we shouldn't grieve. What's gone is gone, the past is done with. I shall cherish the memory, not cast it out of my heart, but there is no return!'

He just stood there staring at his amputated leg with a moronic stare, having a grudge against the world. After having that dreadful and dire episode, he had started his studies again with an air of great expectation and curiosity. He burst into tears, releasing all his pent-up emotions. The delightful guide of neighbours was his guardian angel when he was in danger.

The criminals he had seen so far around maidan at night were wild and powerful like the forces of nature. All political parties subjected most of the criminals to their slippery ideologies and opinions in a web of intrigue rather than in the real world. Memories of their childhood were hazy and broken up in a complex web of relationships. With a nod and a smile, they didn't give clear answers to a question about why they had not been at home every night. The age-old criminals were so tired that their eyelids were beginning to hang down. Most of them had drunk so much alcohol that they couldn't speak clearly. Freedom was to them a slippery concept because its meaning changed according to a person's point of view. Political scandals have left the reputation of democracy in ruins since independence.

There was very little breeze and the scarlet mushroom hung in the quiet air like a blotch of blood against the pale inter sky. The neighbours had all gone back to their homes. It was a queer situation all round the maidan; a distraught woman, an unconscious child, a drunken husband were seen lurking in the maidan. It was getting colder and colder. He saw some men quite drunk, half numb with a kind of saturated happiness like anguish, a feeling dolorous and pleasant, bruising somewhere, and a drumming of their blood all over their body. All around was peace and quiet, but there was no peace in Mr. Mitra's heart, no clarity in his mind.

Mr. Mitra walked slowly and reluctantly, relying on his walking stick. As he walked on, he recollected the days of his childhood days. With the lapse of years all family differences and squabbles were forgotten, leaving ever more vivid memories of those years when the berry garden had seemed a mysterious and alluring jungle, when he had gone out to the field with his father that first sunny morning walked behind the harrow. Mr. Mitra availed himself of the first convenient pretext for leaving the family.

He walked with a stately sailing motion towards Old People's Home where all of his friends had already got into their own room. He got into the room. There was a wick-lamp burnt in a corner of the room, set about with expensive city-style furniture and numerous indoor plants.

It was eight o'clock in the morning. It had been morning when Mr. Shibnath Mitra had awakened finding himself alone in the room. He spent the morning padding about the room in his slippers. A cold wet morning in which rain fell steadily. He recollected the days of World War II in Calcutta. The city had been filled with panic in those days, as telegram after telegram, message after message, brought news of disaster. Calcutta was bewildered and helpless and apparently unable to do more than protect itself from a peril that had passed from it to spread out like a forest fire over half India. As he walked past a restaurant, he heard an extremely unpleasant and repulsive noise from a restaurant. He stopped for a while, clutching his walking stick. The dusty airless darkness closed in upon. The wrangling voices passed down roads.

Everyone smoked, and very soon the atmosphere was thick and blue. Everyone talked and argued, and presently a man with one leg came in and sat in a corner and began to play an accordion. He didn't play it loudly and the sound only just emerged from among the sea of voices, but there was something in the music which added a touch of colour to the room.

He got to feel, 'the material dependence comes into conflict with independence of spirit. The majority of men are like animals---they take, fright and are reassured by trifles. The enemies always win because of their superior numbers as our age in the superior court of Death.' He flashed out a superior smile.

The air was cold and soft without a breath of wind but there was a gentle stirring all around like the earth itself was breathing softly. When Mr. Mitra got among the trees he couldn't bring himself to start crying out after a tea-seller in a great bawling voice. It would've been like hollering in a holy place. So he just went on walking softly with his walking stick as he was weak and coward. He came himself upon quite by accident. He was sitting at the foot of a big tree just off the main road. His big eyes were watching everything. A political leader was voicing forth electioneering campaign and trying to emphasize his good points sounding boastful in presence of illiterate and rustic villagers hired out from distant villages of West Bengal.

Mr. Mitra sat down with his back to a tree-trunk and tried not to think of a dozen things that he had seen that morning. Things that made his stomach heave and cramp with rage, and a red haze swim in his brain so that some primitive, unreasoning tribal instinct made him, for one dreadful instinct.

He got a strange feeling inside him and he thought how old the tree was for himself, so full of running and leaping and hurling himself about most of the time. He them glanced back toward the maidan. The evergreen sparkled in the bright moonlight and the tall lean birches were like white beckoning fingers. It bid fair to be the coldest day of the year.

A full moon sailed the skies outside. The air flowed in broad tranquil waves, lots of it, filling one's lungs with its exhilarating freshness. The young birches in the clearings sheered fearfully to the side, the slender little pines shook their heads meditatively, the tender branches of the sunflowers quivered, and the little fir trees stretched their fluffy branches out trustingly like childish hands with outspread fingers. He stood there, looking at the awe-inspiring and breath-taking beauty of nature.

He avidly listened to a melodious voice from a bungalow not far away from his old people's home where all boarders were singularly foolish. At this age, none was solidly behind him. A cunning intellect was patiently diverting every circumstance. He felt a strong, very unpleasant smell of treachery hung in the air. He held his breath as a rat scuttled past.

From a nearby bungalow came a burst of atmospheric music, and the words of a hymn creating an exciting mood:

'If you believe, your dreams will all come true,

Embrace the Lord, and he will see you through,

If you have faith, there's nothing you can't do.'

Mr. Mitra listened to the receding song and gazed at the blue sky. He buried his face in his hands and sobbed aloud. He spoke to himself: 'Where there's change there will always be resistance. That's dialectics.' He inclined his head in a slight but gracious nod of dismissal and turned his attention to the elderly companions.

His eyes bulged in their eyes. Even with his head hunched deep into his shoulder and his eyes narrowed to tiny slits, it was hopeless to penetrate into the hymn. A star dropped athwart the skyline, leaving a momentary glowing trail in its wake. He loved this world of big skies and quiet maidan where man was so dear that every person met by chance along the boundless track of maidan.

Having a brazen boldness coupled with impudent assurance and insolence, the age-old persons departed the maidan. A galaxy of stars was found throughout the universe. He muttered in soft voice: 'The day has declined and let us go fetch water. Her white feet scorched by the heat. Knee-deep she stood in the water.'

He often said to his friends, taking sudden, sharp breaths: 'In old age, all people live in cages---Cages of good behaviour and decent manners. A cage is none the worse for being gilded. A man in a foreign country is like a mad dog. In old age, we take too much upon ourselves. By what right?—and by what right? And why in the name of the four hundred and ninety-nine thousand angels,' thought he impatiently, as he had thought so often before, 'can I not rid myself of this habit of seeing both sides of a thing instead of only my own? Which is my

own?' He laughed unconcernedly as he heard some slum-children crying noisily, in an annoying way.

He felt rather cold. His hair had worn off. When he was young, he was a powerfully made young man with broad shoulders and long legs and a quiet walk. Outside he was beautifully and splendidly dressed, but inside he was an empty walnut. Remorse was his daily portion in this land of dreams. He was looking none too thrilled. None but he knew many untold happenings behind this old historical maidan.

As they left the maidan, the uncultivated and uninhabited tract of Brigade Parade Ground seemed to have slept in remote wilderness of space groups of nebulae. He went right to the place where the house had been on fire.

Mr. Mitra stood there, looking fixedly at the half-burnt house with wide-open eyes and relying on the crutches putting under his arms. As he abruptly turned off his face, he saw a tall woman, verging on old age, with a coldly handsome face and smooth loops of light brown hair already lightly streaked with grey. He heard her words and watched her with special attention. He had not had time to speak to her before the meeting, but he knew his suspicion of everything unverified and untested as well as he knew his ability, once that suspicion was overcome, of tackling a new meeting with characteristic sweep and enthusiasm.

She was standing apart by the nearest banyan tree, using it as a shelter against the scorching heat of the sun and wind evidently waiting, until the major portion of the crowd had left. Something about her that attracted him was that he had the impression that he knew her, or had seen her before. As he reached there, he heard the agonized moaning of an age-old woman. Listening to the moans Mr. Mitra wondered why the Almighty had thought fit to inflict on womankind such a lengthy and agonizing method of populating the earth. And why, in the name of God the Merciful and Compassionate, had this got to happen now?

She stood quite still: so still that he suddenly realized when and where it was that he had seen her. His craggy face furrowed into a look of acute bewilderment. He stood for so long without moving that Sanjukta began to feel uncomfortable. He had not seen her since the day she married. He put his hands into his pockets.

There was a lengthy pause. He came up the side steps and got back to her. He trod with the long, firm and rather heavy strides, relying on his steel-made crutches, of a man accustomed too much walking. He became at once the cynosure of general friendly attention.

Sanjukta was a pleasant woman with a somewhat anxious manner, and saw the four slum-children, wrapped in torn-shawls, lay asleep in the arms of a pale-cheeked old woman. By a combination of diet and exercise Sanjukta had become smaller in size from 70 kilos to 50. She seated herself on the hard ground with her back to a tree trunk a few yards where Mr. Mitra had taken up his stand and she took off her wide-brimmed hat and let the faint breeze ruffle her hair. She wanted to go up and have a heart-to-heart talk to him, but he had a crowd round him and she remained seated where she was in an irresolute, undecided, and hesitating manner.

Sanjukta stood quite still: so still that he suddenly realized when and where it was that he had seen her. It was the woman who had instigated her father to get his leg amputated. Something about her attracted Mr. Mitra's attention, for despite the heavy veil that obscured her features he had the impression that he knew her, or had seen her before.

Her two children had both been born, lived their brief days and died in this country, and had been laid to rest in Calcutta. She saw Calcutta as the graveyard of her children; a country with a medieval standard of morality, sanitation and squalor. Political leaders got used to spilling communal tension over into other areas of Calcutta. She was quite unmindful of people moving impetuously, violently, and angrily through the streets.

He said nothing but she sensed the struggle in him. There was a fluttering in the pit of her stomach and her palms were moist. In the distance a loon laughed hysterically. A bat wheeled through the dusk of the maidan. On the crest of a big tree to the west, two cocoanut trees, towering above their neighbours in black silhouette thrust ragged spears into the belly of the night. The last of the day's light in a suffusion of pale blood flowed into the horizon. Mr. Mitra said, 'There's a talk.'

Sanjukta moistened her lips and tried to keep her voice easy. 'Talk about us. They're saying'….they're saying you cannot keep on here much longer.'

'Yes…I have heard.'

'Is it true?'

'I…I don't know, Shibnath.'

He suddenly slammed his fists together and said; 'They got no right!'

The naked desperation in his voice made her want to put her arms around him and comfort him. He took his fists apart and studied his hands. His monkish clotted hair stood out around his face. He was staring up from the ground at Sanjukta. He remembered that fine beautiful face somehow framed, still in medieval grace, in gently contoured hair, over the white brow, over the ears, caught back of the head in a knot.

He then said, 'They're saying the kid needs a father.' Everything happened to him in an unusual and amusing way. He then leaned against a tree. A little stripped squirrel which had crept within a yard of his feet whisked away with an indignant chirr. An intense shivery sensation of fear got into his mind. A few short-lived insects were smoothly walking over his foot. He made a rude gesture at them, standing off.

Looking at some splashes on his shirt, she hesitantly held out a thin white hand with a gesture that was almost royal, and Mr. Shibnath Mitra bowed over it and straightened up to meet the critical gaze of a pair of slightly prominent black eyes, cold, pale and calculating. The noise of the running vehicles drove him crazy. His heart was beating by and large and trying to behave normally. In spite of walking difficulties, he was rubbing along the walking stick. He tried forgetting his old romance as his age was getting on eighty. That romance with Sanjukta had been boisterously carefree, joyful, and high-spirited like a rollicking adventure film. He felt a tumultuous disturbance in mind. The crowd, going past them, instantly diverted and turned to see who it was who the lady had greeted.

Raising his sunken eyes, he said softly, looking into her eyes, 'Sanjukta! You are here! It's quite unbelievable! Why are you here?' She was wearing a run-down sari. His calling withered her with a look. He tried to turn around quickly and stepped on his walking-stick.

A long silence fell between them. They exchanged furtive glances. The day was unusually cold and sunny for the time of year, with the temperature in thirties. The month might have been August were it not for the angle of the sunshine slanting through the trees and casting the long shadows of houses across the dusty roads getting down past the maidan. Inevitably the past became shadowy and unreal to Sanjukta. Mr. Mitra stood where he was, swaying a little and breathing heavily, staring only at her gloomy eyes. She didn't know that her father had had his leg amputated when he wanted to get ahead in his career.

He muttered: 'Thank you, Sanjukta, for your father's gift---a free gift for my romance. Your father was then giddy with happiness as my leg was amputated. Your father trampled on the rights of others. Every romance lies between death and disaster. Let a fool have to do with foolish things. Your father dies but his influence remains.' He tossed his head angrily, having had his lesson of romance. He cursed his folly and blamed himself for his foolishness. He had a pain down his amputated leg.

'You're very angry, aren't you? What do you say muttering?' asked Sanjukta uncertainly. Her voice was trailing off.

Mr. Mitra only gave a charming smile and felt a kind of wonder singing inside him. He visualized her face as he talked to her. She looked at him with her funny soft smile he could never quite explain. He felt the sudden rush of anger that always seized him at the prospect of a fight.

Both Mr. Mitra and Mrs. Sanjukta suddenly watched an ambulance, making a long loud sound as a warning, was getting past them, carrying a burning patient. They stepped forward when the ambulance raced past with its siren above the roar of the crowd. They noticed that a tall, young handsome boy was chasing away the ambulance with a loud voice, 'Nandita! Nandita! I'm coming, coming soon, Nandita! I'm with you! Don't worry, Nandita.' He was having a romantic relationship with her, looking at the bright side of his future. She was 20 at college. Vivacious and animated in spirit, she got used to having a day out with that young handsome boy born of educated parents.

His heart-felt agony had stirred the silent spectators standing around the pavements. The encroaching settlers displaced the native peoples and accused of invading their privacy. Four grizzled beard elderly persons of Old People's Homes felt aggrieved at his high-pitched agony, looking at him with an absent stare.

The sizeable pavement dwellers, living in abysmal conditions of poverty, witnessed the whole incident in one sitting. Their unfed and unroofed kids, playing on waste ground behind a tea-stall, stood aghast. They grouped themselves around them, making a continuous rough and grating noise.

Mr. Mitra's eyes kept straying into some street-dogs that, in all shapes and sizes, avoiding barking were seen sitting together and looking silently at the moving ambulance. They felt embarrassed as they stared blankly at the young, handsome boy, running as fast as he could behind the ambulance, carrying his warm and loving word 'Nandita, my heart!' Mr. Mitra and Mrs. Sanjukta couldn't get a grip on what was going on around her. Mr. Mitra stood keeping a quiet steady attitude, like a seasoned veteran, amidst the sedentary birds flying over his head.

As the time went on, Mrs. Sanjukta grew more and more impatient to know around her and said to him: 'Everything happened to come before my eyes. Do you hear there is a groundswell of opinion that their romance is deep?'

Looking at her weather-beaten face, Mr. Mitra said: 'Ooh! If every one of us is going to shun people what will be our life like? You're a woman of experience and culture, Sanjukta, look what your father did to me. Who escapes from the net of woman? Love perfumes the night and flourishes under grave. I'm here today, tomorrow, and the day after; but the next, I will die. Every old person is like the boat in death-bed.'

'I know it. Forgive me, Shibnath. I can't understand what you say,' said Sanjukta briskly, staring at him. She got flushed with anger. After a persistent request, he said:

'The boat is at the bank, but there is no boatman!' said he. His heart was aching for those young boys hankering after suitable partners as romance was quite farce to him.

Sanjukta said, wringing her hands: 'Everybody can sew and sing, but sewing and singing are the arts in which everyone cannot be perfect. Time heals griefs and quarrels, for we change and are no longer the same persons.' She sighed as a voiceless crying of old love that died and never spoke. She fixed her eyes in a steady intent look at the maidan with studious attention. The maidan—a vast stretch of field—is referred to as the Brigade Parade Ground. She knew: 'it includes Eden Gardens, several football stadiums. The wide field stretches from the Hooghly River in the west to the Victoria Memorial in the east.'

Mr. Mitra cast a glance at her and said: 'I know we are only in falsehood, duplicity, contradiction; we both conceal and disguise ourselves from ourselves. Can you tell me who prays to God in happiness, how sorrow can come?'

Sanjukta looked sullen and silent, looking at some undernourished elderly persons sitting together down the pavement where treachery was lying underneath a mask of friendliness in the city of Calcutta where peace litters

with corruption. She gestured with fingers spread in mock, desperation, her glance mocked out of the corners of her eyes.

The white cloth which had once covered Nandita was gone, and the sodden, bloodstained blanket was torn half through and hanging loose. One end of it had been dragging in the mud and only the once white towels with which he had tried to staunch the flow of bold covered the lower half of her body. The chalk white limbs were bruised and lacerated and even her blouse and brassiere had been half torn. One of his shoes was missing; the other was like a huge club foot packed into a great lump of black mud. His blond hair was matted with grime and leaves. Upset and distressed in mind, that young boy crying aloud was laying his head on the bloodstained blanket.

Looking at her face, he said with an intense pain of mind, 'Nandita! Nandita! Please talk to me. Open your eyes, Nandita. Don't leave me alone, Nandita. I can't live without you. This that you have witnessed shall be binding upon all.' He had always wanted to paint a sunrise with Nandita.

The water ran him off making a muddy red pool at his feet, as he stood desperately gripping the limp body of his beloved girl. The young boy didn't know that his beloved Nandita had already died on the way to hospital. No sooner had the ambulance reached the hospital than the young boy came close to Nandita lying dead on the bed. Her lips were yielding; she didn't respond but she was not unfriendly. He kissed her, and the success went to his head. He put his arms about her and drew her towards him and tried to kiss her again. Her lips sunk deeply between his arms while he made her head loll back over his arm. The water ran in a steady stream from her tangled hair on his arm and her face had that faintly greenish hue of a corpse. The rows of watching men swayed and bowed and groveled in a state of half-hypnotic frenzy. The whole picture was something out of a nightmare.

There were some dazed and terrified people herded together like sheep in that courtyard of hospital. And towards evening half a dozen elderly men of low caste who acted as sweepers and disposers of filth, heaped the stiffened, mangled bodies on to cars which dragged them to the burial ground. Looking at

them, a boarder of Old People's Home said in a cold voice: 'All elderly people suffer from a hysterical mania for cleanliness and sanctity. This has been happening down the ages always. We are alone, like a leper. Umm! What I have seen at this age!'

And then he suddenly felt that his 'Nandita' had already left her last breath. After the first scream, he had stood frozen. He stood beside her, crying aloud, putting a hand upon her arm and giving a graceful bow to her. Her death had taught him how to be gracious in defeat. The passers-by stood aghast at the sight of a horrible scene, and the boarders of Old People's Home, looking out the windows, heard a bubbling, angst-ridden cry of a young boy, shrill and high and almost instantly drowned in the concerted groaning howl of the crowd standing off the ambulance. He heard the distant creaks and groans echoed eerily along the dark corridors of morgue.

The huge stone-paved courtyard of the hospital lay bathed in starlight in which the clumps of coarse grass and stunted saplings had thrust up here and there between the paving stones took on the appearance of crouching men. The two men stole forward silently to the morgue, moving from one clump of shadow to the next, and reached the morgue.

As the news of her death came to them at night, the elderly persons got shocked. The news was extremely startling, distressing and offensive to the local inhabitants. They were all shocked at the news of her death. Having got the news, Mr. Mitra got a terrible shock, looking shockingly ill. He knew them well.

With bated breath, he spoke to himself:' their ill-fated romance ultimately ended into disaster. Unblessed is he who dies in bed of romance as our sons and daughters-in-law insulted their parents by contemptuous facial expression or tone of voice. It is the comedy of many life situations. There is not a trace of truth in what I think. Calcutta is a city with a split personality.'

Next day afternoon, Mr. Mitra gave the news of her death to the community of his retired friends, sitting together in a lush green field, making

them feel pleasure to know their romance. He related the story of their romance:

'The boy was a professional killer at the age of twenty-three. He fell in love with an innocently-looking luscious village girl coming from Purulia. She was quite literate. Crabbed age and youth cannot live together. I heard she looked particularly lovely on her death-bed. Love was a word that didn't come easily to him, but I knew he loved her with a force so strong that everything else in life paled by comparison. We're not living in easy circumstances....' He looked at a litter of puppies lying asleep on the pavement strewn with waste papers and filthy materials.

There was a continuous noise of quacking and quarrelling birds and the ruffle of wings made a soothing and monotonous music. The bright moonlight chequered the maidan with patters of light and shade, and the sky no longer appeared to weigh down upon the wide maidan as it seemed sometimes to do in the heat of the day, but to curve high and cool and cloudless; as full of peace and serenity as the placid maidan.

Saying so, he lowered his voice to a sigh. His friends also lowered their own head. Surprised and worried about her death, Mr. Mitra said: 'Good Lord, what you have done to them!' His face wrinkled into a smile. He suddenly heard the sound of a man's voice, faintly familiar and speaking in tones of cold rage:

'---so all are endangered!'

'Nay, all are now bound one to another!' replied another in a shrill, hysterical voice

His friends stayed silent. There was a brief silence. The tragic episode silenced them in honour of a young girl who had left the young boy into an awkward silence. And their long sigh resounded through maidan like a thousand vanquished men in a bloody fight. All of them stood up for a three-minute silence. His close friend, crippled with arthritis, was no longer able to walk normally. His eyes gleamed in the starlight, and he struggled hard to rise to his one foot with the walking stick. He came to him and buried his weeping face into his hands.

'I wish to sing along if I know the words, Mr. Mitra,' said he in tearful eyes. He let the breath out of his lungs slowly, then reached out and took the cigarettes without taking his eyes off the police. He began searching his pockets for a match. Another friend, aged about 69, snapped a lighter and held it. Again there was a tiny hesitation from Mr. Mitra before he leaned forward and lit the tobacco.

His eyes were acutely suspicious. He inhaled deeply, blew the smoke out through his nostrils and extended the package. As they were ready to get back home, lowering their head to get through the street, they heard a few men conferred together in whispers: 'It is late, and I have far to go before morning.' It was the same voice that Mr. Mitra had heard screaming shrilly of death. Mr. Mitra stared for so long that the stub of his cigarette burnt his fingers. He stared, dropped it and ground it out beneath his shoe.

Next day all of his elderly persons arrived at the maidan for an evening walk. As the sun went down, a dog was barking mournfully from the plain beyond the maidan and a little breeze rustled through the surrounding scrub, whispering through the leaves of the peepul tree and filling the silent evening with a hundred small stealthy sounds in a lovely and cold city. The evening breeze had tugged unexpectedly at the light shawl that Sanjukta wore and had tangled its long silk fringe about a stanchion, and Mr. Mitra, who had been passing, had come to her assistance. She had thanked him prettily. His gaze had fallen upon her ring finger. She had been wearing her husband's ring--- the great carved emerald in the curious setting.

The pupils of his eyes had narrowed like a cat's in the light, and he said in his soft voice whose faintly sing-song intonation alone betrayed the fact. He spoke: 'That is a very unusual ring you are wearing. May I be permitted to ask where it came from? It looks as though it were a jewel from England.'

'Perhaps it is,' said Sanjukta, holding it out for him to see. She lifted one of the rough, worn hands, kissed it swiftly and rose to her feet. She laced her fingers behind her head.

'That is very interesting,' said Mr. Mitra, looking at her, 'Can we take our own road from here?'

Mr. Mitra raised his brows at her, 'Why not? Let's go on, madam.'

Sanjukta glowed at him and said: 'You have got the most poisonous tongue of any woman I know. By God, I don't know why I put up with you!'

'Because I am a habit with you, and you have never been able to break yourself of bad habits,' said Mrs. Sanjukta laughed her low and throaty laugh.

Mr. Mitra was an agreeable man and entertaining conversationalist.

Looking at them, Mrs. Sanjukta said,' I saw the hundreds of streets, the countless houses, the innumerable wealth and the splendour of Calcutta thirty years ago. But the mental make-up of people has not yet changed. The people of Calcutta should know how to colour their nature well. The majority of them only know how to be a great hypocrite and dissembler.'

Much to his surprise he grew enthusiastic, smiled, frowned and twitched his eyebrows with such vigour that his grey crop of hair on his head began to stir. Sanjukta was fair and pure as a lily that had bloomed in Paradise.

She marveled how she could ever have been wrought upon to marry him! She deemed it her crime most to be repented of, that she had ever endured, and reciprocated, the lukewarm grasp of his hand, and had suffered the smile of her lips and eyes to mingle and melt into his own. He had persuaded her to fancy herself happy by his side.

She had liked his smile too, the broad embarrassed smile of a man who rarely smiled. The year's experience had shown how happy they had been after thirty-five years. She lowered her newspaper having no connection with serious

artistic and cultural ideas. She looked around the maidan where the lights were low and romance was in the air in a lively, quick tone.

She drew his attention to look at the Old People's Home where she was living. He stayed there, gazing at the Old People's Home. Some went somewhere secretly, trying to avoid being seen, because it was unpleasant to live in, unclean and unhealthy. They stood at the coffee shop. The coffee steamed up out of the cup and she held her face above it, mum, well, but the first sip was too hot, she let it wait a minute.

Mrs. Sanjukta touched her cup of coffee with a thoughtful finger, up and down the curve, but the heat was hotter, swelling; it was fear swelling inside her. Across the other side, the hall was dark, and even the doors. She muttered: 'Everyone should look into the mirror once a week. Deadly snakes spit and hiss when they are cornered.' She saw the wind had broken a tree in two. Clear with the hazy clearness that promised a day of grinding heat.

After a persistent request, Mr. Mitra agreed to go to her room. Her room was not designed to let air and some light in, but to keep out strong sunlight or rain. There was a passage from here to the dining room. Living alone in an Old People's Home, she recollected the scene that had taken place between them the day of her arrival in Science College and the arguments he had used to persuade her, and she continued silly with a secret smile: 'Why don't you want to understand? There's no love lost between you and me. I was much loved by all who knew me in college days. For the love of God, tell me what I was wrong with you! You haven't told me the story behind your leg amputated. Tell me what happened to you.' He only turned his face back, standing only a foot away.

The room reeked of sickness and resounded with Sanjukta's lamentations. Her maidservant was stout, brisk and motherly, and had once been a nursemaid. She had borne and lost several children in Calcutta, but sorrow and adversity did not appear to have damped her invincible spirits, and after a year spent in Delhi, to which she had returned in the capacity of nurse to the invalid old widow.

She often said to Sanjukta, 'If you don't keep anything down, you will keep on bringing nothing up, and that's uncomfortable as well I know. The worst people today are very rude and insulting, and intended to damage a woman's reputation by slanderous rumours.' She then left Sanjukta with quick short steps.

Her energetic ministrations had the desired effect. He was silent, and preoccupied, almost sullen. He looked around her. The maidan were thick with wild flowers and the air so heavy with their scent it was difficult to breathe. If you listened very closely you could hear the steady hum of bees beneath the shrill piping of the birds. Some Muslim pavement dwellers were lying under the open sky. In the hot weather many men slept out in the open, in roadways and on rooftops and at the doors of their huts. How many would have seen the red comet, and how many—or how few?—would not regard it as a sign from heaven?

They stared up at the blaze of stars through the mosquito nets, and saw a comet cross the heavens from east to west, not with the rush of a falling star, but slowly, drawing a long train of glowing light that appeared red rather than white or golden, and taking a full ten minutes to traverse the spangled ceiling of the sky. From a dozen yards to his left he heard an age old Muslim move and looking in his direction saw the silhouette of his lifted head and knew that he had seen it, too.

A red star was smearing a trail of blood from the east to the west. Were there such things as signs and wonders in the sky? A star had once brought Wise Men out of the East to search for that Sword that had come into the world so many centuries ago and had not yet been sheathed. That the heavens foretold the future was perhaps the oldest superstition in the world, and men had watched the skies for ten thousand years or more, believing that their fate could be read there. An evil sign: not because of its colour, for red is worn in the East for rejoicing, but because the times and men's thoughts were evil.

'They have seen it,' Mr. Mitra thought. 'This is how legends are born.'

'Please could you speak more slowly?' said Mrs. Sanjukta with a forced smile. He didn't reply but a tricky glance at her. Her blouse had come undone. Everything was undone by age.

The red-tailed comet sank behind the mango trees, its reflection lingering for a moment longer in the dark maidan, and as the glow faded from the sky the dogs stopped howling as though at an order. The moonlight did not disguise the dark colour that showed briefly in Mr. Shibnath Mitra's face. He caught the mockery in her tone, glanced at her, saw the laughing black eyes, and recalled that he had argued with her thirty-five years ago in exactly the same words and smiled despite himself. He saw her quick breath of relief, and smiled.

But innate good nature kept his mouth sealed and looked at the north field of the maidan, inspecting the possible places where her father with other miscreants had beaten him and made his leg amputated in a long rainy season. He had nothing to say on that score. She didn't raise her eyes from him and asked: 'What are you looking at, in this sumptuous evening, Shibnath?'

Looking at him, Mrs. Sanjukta muttered: 'As a man who had once sinned, but who kept his conscience all alive and painfully sensitive by the fretting of an unhealed wound, he might have been supposed safer within the line of virtue, than he had never sinned at all.'

'Nothing at all, Sanjukta,' said Shibnath in an agreeably smooth and silken voice, giving a significant glance at her. It sounded, suddenly, entirely natural and reasonable, and no longer some dark and mysterious and unexplainable process fraught with terror and uncertainty.'

The sweat ran down his face and blinded his eyes, and Mrs. Sanjukta flinched and gasped at every scream, but Mr. Mitra's voice remained steady and reassuring and Mrs. Sanjukta's eyes clung desperately to his---as desperately as her hands.

As they were looking at each other after the long shadows of separation, a village girl was seen going past them, singing a song. Her musical voice, as soothing as south-wind, rang clear in the evening:

'A shining star fell from above

And lit up all around,

I kissed and hugged the lad I love,

My heart began to pound.'

Mr. Mitra and Mrs. Sanjukta joined in the song, standing on the dry parched grass. The melody floated and melted upon the air. They looked at the myriad stars that flowed and twinkled overhead, spinning an endless gleaming web in the throbbing sky. The air around them began to stir, it rustled as the wings of eagles rustle, and it took life. Her bright eyes gazed upon him, strange whispers shook his soul. Upon the darkness were bars of light. They changed and interchanged; they moved to and fro and wove mystic symbols which Mr. Mitra couldn't read. Sorrow was piled on sorrow. Splendor heaped on splendour's head. He provided it in cold silence that was a thousand times worse than defiance.

He thought within himself: 'How sweet from a full heart of love she sings her message to her dear! Indeed it is a lovely evening, and most beautiful is Nature's music, sung with a hundred voices from wind and trees and birds and ocean's wrinkled lips, and yet sung all to tune. Never to have loved—it is strange! Never to have known some woman-heart beat all in tune to you---never to have seen the eyes of your adored swim with passion's tears, as the girl sighed her vows upon her breast! ---never to have loved! ---nor to have lost yourself in the mystery of another's soul; nor to have learned how Nature can overcome our naked loneliness, and with the golden web of love of twain weave one identity! Her mental faculties remain unimpaired.'

As Mr. Mitra murmured she drew near to him, till at last, with a long, sweet sigh, looking at his walking stick. She flung one arm about his neck, and gazed upon him with unfathomable eyes, and smiled her dark, slow smile that, like an opening flower, revealed beauty hidden. Her perfumed breath played upon his wrinkled cheek. He kept turning over the events of the day in his mind.

Looking at her bright-shinning eyes, he felt: 'Woe is me! Love is always secret and mysterious and therefore difficult to understand. Marriage is, by turns, funny and very sad.' He saw hundreds of elderly persons had already left the maidan. The sky was constantly varying. The weather became so bad that they had to turn back home. But he became too concerned with his own problems and stopped communicating with others.

His full mouth was fresh and smiling, outlined by the surrounding grey hair. He had seen her last thirty-five years ago. When he stood before the mirror, the wrinkles truly showed him the warning to leave from this most evil world with the vilest worms to dwell.

The last echoes of her rich notes had floated down the college campus, and slowly died away; but in his heart they had rolled on and on. Never had he heard one so thrilling or so sweet with passion's honey-notes. Her sweet voice still ran parallel to her surpassing grace and loveliness of her beauty.

He came into consciousness as she said, 'You are her, Shibnath!'

He was startled by her question, and looked at her with surprising eyes. Looking at her, he mumbled, 'your presence in my sight awakes my heart to heart's and eye's delight. Despite of wrinkles, you must die single, and my love will die with me.' He then forced his voice to a more conciliatory tone.

'Yes, I'm Shibnath,' said he laconically, looking at her unforgotten eyes, thin lips, and bewitching eyes, 'The pulp of a green coconut tastes sweeter than the kernel of a ripe one.' He suddenly got a pleasant noticeable smell of coffee from a nearby coffee-making shop and said: 'Do you have a cup of coffee?'

She suddenly burst into tears. She, biting her lips on her tears, finally agreed with what he had said. He was flustered. His fresh-skinned face coloured up. He glanced about and gave a gusty sigh. They got to the coffee-shop and had two cups of coffee in presence of some criminals and hired murderers. On the other side of the street, they heard music blared from the open window of the house. But before the morning was out he knew with a sick despair that he would not allow to show in his face that he was fighting a losing battle.

His face was marred by sorrow; his tangled hair, grizzled with years, hung about his hollow eyes, and white on his chin was the stubble of an unshaven beard. His robe was squalid, and his aspect more wretched than that of the poorest beggar at the temple gates. He turned off his head as he heard the sound of stir and bustle in the maidan. A moonlight picnic in the maidan had been arranged by the livelier spirits among the young drunkards.

Someone in the picnic pulled the elderly person back, and the knife flashed and fell. There was a bubbling, agonized cry, shrill and high and almost instantly drowned in the concerted groaning howl of participants. But it had not been an animal's cry, and Mr. Mitra stumbled to his feet with his walking stick and stood against the slimy stone of the pillar, and saw what it was that had cried out. They didn't know what misfortune was waiting for them, and they were wasting time uttering social inanities. They left the place in fear.

She remained soundless, looking at him with a simpering smile. Her head ached from the intense cold pressing against her temples. Her nose was running and there was excruciating pain now in her cheeks and ears. The temperature was getting lower and lower. Her fingers were numb. She looked at him. He had his face on his walking stick. His nose, too, was running and his face was raw. She was conscious only of an unfamiliar and inexplicable feeling of being safe: a feeling she had been a stranger to ever since the day when a small, weeping and bewildered child had been torn from the comforting arms of her mother.

'I couldn't understand why you said so, Shibnath,' said Sanjukta in wonder. Her expression changed but she didn't make exclamations of pity or admiration. She paused, hesitated, and smiled. He shook his head. His attitude, had Mrs. Sanjukta known it, was entirely genuine. The sight of Mrs. Sanjukta's scarlet cheeks and wide, horrified eyes brought home to Mr. Mitra for the first time.

'Do you come here to make my other leg amputated, Sanjukta?' asked he in a supple voice, staring at her face with an enquiring mind, 'I'm ready at any time. Do not keep me waiting.'

'Why do you say so, Shibnath?' asked Sanjukta with tearful eyes

'Some men look at the elderly persons with sanctimonious reverence. We feel wanting in our humdrum lives. At this age, we are deluded and then disillusioned cynicism and confusion.'

Her cheeks were suddenly wet with tears, and she bent and kissed his hand, released him and stood up. The shamed colour faded from Mrs. Sanjukta's cheeks, and the horror in her eyes was replaced by interest. Now he waited for an answer, waited with an acuteness which made him sweat. There was a moistening of her lips, slight quiver of the throat muscles preparing words. But there was no alteration of the vacant evading face.

Weary and spent with fears and the pangs of guilt, his heart sought her for rest, for now she alone was left to me. He recollected the past episode that had happened thirty-five years ago. He was courageously resolute in the face of difficulty. Her father had grounded down his love with his daughter by years of negligence. He stood off a garden that had been grassed over.

He was immersed in deep thought and began to think over the past days: 'She sworn to wed him, and with the treasure we won we would make our marriage strong and I would free her from her foes. How fair she seemed, even in her disarray, her long hair streaming down her breast! How deadly fair she seemed in the faint light—this woman the story of whose beauty and whose sin shall outlive the solid mass of the mighty British imperialism predominated over us! Ah! Could I have seen the picture that was to come, how, and in what place and circumstance, once again this very woman's head should be laid upon my knee, pale with that cast of death! Ah! Could I have seen! '

The heaviness of her swoon had smoothed away the falseness of her face, and nothing was left but the stamp of Woman's richest loveliness, softened by the shadows of the night and dignified by the cast of deathlike sleep.

Mr. Mitra took a step forward, bracing against the wind, and as he did so there was a light pain somewhere. His amputated legs felt hot and wet. He looked down. The little porch was flooded with blood. He stared at it,

unbelievingly. The colour began to drain from his face. 'Oh! God! Oh, dear merciful God! Have mercy on me! Please!' He felt uncomfortable. Sanjukta got confused a little. A few moments later, he got steady as he was before, leaning on the outworn walking stick. He smiled at her.

He glanced at her and saw that she was confused, for her eyes shone and her bosom heaved. So, he sighed and kissed at her shrunken cheek, setting the seal upon his shame and bondage. A change—life came back to him.

His voice was as tritely astonished as a pair of raised eyebrows, the intonation of surprise employed when, knowing what Sanjukta did mean, he would yet extract from her, to make her knowledge his existence, monosyllabic replies, reluctant explanations, sentences as brief as she could keep them. He thus extracted, from her taciturnity like a blank back turned upon him, a reassurance of their relationship. He strove to come close to her by a bridge of syllables; forcing her to break with speech the solitude she imposed by her presence at his side.

'You must forgive me for the heinous crime done to you,' said Sanjukta curtly, 'but I wished to see you privately. I have something to say to you that your friends would apparently prefer to remain unsaid. I took this method of ensuring that you would see me.'

He saw the slender figure stiffen and draw itself erect, and the dark eyes became guarded. 'What is it you wish to tell me?'

Mr. Mitra studied her for a moment, frowning. 'How old are you?' he enquired abruptly. And she answered in unconscious obedience to the authority in his voice. 'I'm seventy five. But I shall soon----'

The unexpectedness of the question appeared to take her by surprise.

'Seventy- five!' said Mr. Mitra exasperated. 'It's not decent. Do you have any conception as to what you say? At this age, you have to go to an Old People's Home.' His voice was hard and expressionless. Sanjukta heard the familiar tongue with a renewal of his previous anger.

A flood of joy, emotion and gratitude towards him swept over her. Looking at his amputated leg and relying on crutches, she wept quiet, acrid, heart-corroding tears, but she didn't weep long. Her sorrow dissolved in the general joy. She understood the implied meaning of his words. A hot wave of new love and gratitude swept over her at the thought of Mr. Shibnath Mitra who had protected her in student life, and it was with a wave of new profound compassion that she gazed at Mr. Mitra's temple.

The joy of victory was interwoven with the joy of a new emotion that took possession of Mrs. Sanjukta Das. Not having once touched her shrunken hand and dried up face, Sanjukta was his first romance in student life in that congeniality, that affinity of characters, feelings and attitudes which was securely established between them. Sanjukta, for the first time as it were, came to know the fullness of family life. She went about subdued with happiness and seemed to have grown younger.

The local neighbours had long since ceased having doubts about the intimacy of two elderly persons, yet they were still afraid to touch each other, studiously calling each other by their first names and sometimes even lapsed into the formal mode of address, dropping the familiar 'you'.

She knew that he yearned for her, but didn't approach her because he was infinitely tender of her feelings, because he was shy of her and afraid to disturb and lose that atmosphere of trust, solicitude and unuttered but brimming tenderness that had sprung up between them.

Sanjukta was still silent, but her silence was as devoid of tension as her body, and the familiar sense of safety and reassurance that his presence could bring to her gradually smoothed out the turmoil in Sanjukta's mind. She glanced uneasily over his shoulder as though to make sure that there could be no third person near them. She had always been a believer in the old saying that it is darkest under the lamp.

Raising her face, she asked him, 'How are you? How did your leg amputated?' Her voice was barely a breath of sound. He was silent for a moment or two, his eyes ranging along the deserted maidan.

He kept himself in total silence. He knew silence was the supreme mystery beyond thought. His deafening silence got her confused. She repeated the questions, but he didn't answer.

After a pause, Mr. Mitra said in a generous and friendly way, 'How lovely to see you after thirty-five years!' He said further, 'We have had a lovely evening in maidan. Family life is the most mysterious location. All that happens in my life is to mould me into a better person.' He only looked at his amputated leg.

'Gracious thanks be to the King of Love for this small mercy,' he answered, looking at her strangely. 'Now, enough of wit come forth upon the maidan---tell me of the mystery of those stars of mine, For I always loved the stars, that are so pure, bright and cold, and so far away from our fevered trouble. Give me of your wisdom and open these wonders to me, for I have little knowledge. Yet my heart is large, and I would fill it, for I have the wit, could I but find the teacher.' A melancholy monotone beat on his heart. A painful thought was flooding in his mind.

Tense silence reigned on his face for a few moments. The evening received him like an over-attentive and slightly sinister friend; its damp embrace cloyed, and he pulled off his muffler as soon as he was in the lane. There was no air, only a drifting mist which had to be breathed in wet and breathed out in a finer form as if the moisture had been refined into steam.

After a thought, he answered back her question. 'I have to tell you later on, Sanjukta,' said he in spongy voice, 'Do you know man is more ferocious than that of the dense forest of the Sundarbans that abound with various kinds of ferocious animals like tigers, hyenas etc.?' He tried to win favour and confidence by imperceptible degrees.

Sanjukta only stared at him without uttering a word. She knew he intentionally insinuated doubts into her trusting mind. She put off her glass and studied it. She suddenly saw a tall, shapely woman, looking younger than her years, in a sari of Indian inspiration by Worth, the lovely throat rising from the gold-trimmed square blouse. Her hair, showing darker in the photograph than in real life, was piled up in loose curls on top of her head. Her hand rested lightly on her age-old husband's sleeve.

Mrs. Sanjukta closely observed the woman. She barely acknowledged her. She seemed to be Kumudini Sen, daughter of an influential tycoon. Mrs. Sanjukta remembered those glorious days in college life. Kumudini Sen herself had been constantly in a state of temptation. Other girls had boasted they'd let boys kiss them or put an arm round them.

Thinking so, Mrs. Sanjukta stepped forward and drew near to her. She said, 'aren't you Kumudini?—yes, I'm Mrs. Kumudini Sen.'

'Who are you?' said Mrs. Kumudini anxiously. Her voice gave Mrs. Sanjukta Das a fascinating insight into her character. Girls around the college had admired her strength of character.

Mrs. Sen, turning off his head, looked at a giant peepul tree split the stones of what had once been a hall of audience, and in the uncertain light it was difficult to tell which were fallen pillars and which the roots of the great tree. He then lowered his hand. He knew what losses and destruction the World War II had caused. The World War II made him realize more vividly and tangibly than ever before the full scale of the war and the heroism of the people who had won it.

'What are you looking at?' said Mrs. Sanjukta in an impertinent and habitual curiosity. Turning off her prematurely white hair, she looked at the most treasured golden bangle given by him thirty years ago.

'I'm looking at the relics of city, madam. Do you know India is full of such ruins; relics of cities and dynasties that have passed away and been forgotten; the haunts of snakes, foxes and monkeys and the lair of the wild boar? A man of

large and scattered property cannot get at it or obtain anything from it. Man is a make-up of mystery,' he said and that in a tone of genial superiority.

Sanjukta noticed both the painful twitch that momentarily transfigured her features and her abrupt withdrawal that resembled flight, but she gave the matter no thought, and was not for a moment diverted from the subject she was on.

A few minutes later, Mrs. Kumudini Sen left the place and was being carried down into heaving darkness to her room of Old People's Home. The room swam unpleasantly before her eyes, and she was forced to lean her aching head against the polished boards.

Mr. Mitra had grown still thinner and paler. The consciousness of his own happiness and well-being evoked in Sanjukta a feeling of sympathy for his vanquished romance. He stood stiffened at the sound of her bluff hearty voice. He encountered her hostile gaze, and smiled. It was a disconcertingly pleasant smile.

He stood staring at the frost-ridden peepul tree that split the stones. Love was a word that didn't come easily to him, but he knew now that he loved her with a force so strong that everything else in life paled by comparison. The fact that she had set a barrier of silence and icy contempt against him filled him with a sick helplessness that not even anger had been able to quench. Each time he had blundered against it, it had grown higher and stronger. He knew she was a daughter of a rich person. The more he fought for her love, the more hopeless his cause had become. And yet he had never admitted it was hopeless.

It had shown Mr. Mitra that sometimes more could be accomplished by keeping his temper in his pocket. It was a momentous conclusion for a man whose approach to every problem had always been a headlong attack.

It was a day filled for her with the bitter sweet of rejoicings and anguish. Mr. Mitra came close to her; his shoulder was touching Sanjukta. She could hear his irregular breathing.

'I have to leave the place now. It is too late to reach the Old People's Home,' said Mitra grimly 'You have to go now. We will not stay here any longer. I'll meet you here tomorrow, Sanjukta.' She jerked herself away from Mr. Mitra's supporting arm, her hand to her mouth and a hot wave of colour dyeing her throat and her pale cheeks.

As they were about to go, they saw an itinerant toy-seller, his pack laden with crudely painted plaster trifles, trudged down the dusty road that led from Dharmatala to Park Street. Leaving Sanjukta behind him, Mr. Mitra was of a cheerful and gregarious disposition and always ready to enter into conversation with fellow travelers upon the road and at the wayside halts.

'Why?' asked she with an inquisitive mind as he insisted on going and was about to turn back towards his destination. He felt an intense pain at his amputated leg. He couldn't express his pain that was uncomfortable with him. She looked at him with an insatiable desire to know about many different things. She came close to him, standing out well against the dark background of maidan. She wished herself a thousand miles away.

'Hm! Half an hour later, this maidan you see will go to the hands of murderous and politically-sponsored unidentified criminals---invisible terrorists of Bengal. The civic society expects no quarter from such a ruthless adversary. The facts are clearly stated in all newspapers. Maidan at night is as slippery and smooth as a serpent. Let's wind up the discussion. This is my telephone no. Take it and call me over phone, if necessary. If you wish really hard, maybe you'll get what you want, Sanjukta.'

She looked very pleased with herself. Her small heart-shaped face was unusually pale, and the shadows under the great eyes made her appear even larger.

Slowly she drew near, bowing as she came. At length she stood before him, and she glanced up. She said, 'It is well; I grew lonely here. Nay, it's a weary world! We know so many faces, and there are so few whom we love to see again. Well, stand not here so mute, but be seated.' Said Sanjukta in a soft

voice, lowering her head down, 'I don't rightly know what I'll say. I feel hesitated.' Mr. Mitra struggled hard to sit on a lush green field. They were seated side by side. Her words were ringing in his ears.

'You seem to be wise beyond your years. Tell me what you want to say, Mrs. Sanjukta,' said Mr. Mitra joyfully, 'Pick the tomatoes before they get to be eaten. It is time that heals every problem.' She lowered her head down. She was clever and efficient but often didn't seem to be sincere.

'Look at that octogenarian old couple is going down the maidan hand in hand. Their gait is slower than expected. They are likely to get to get a blessing from the local temple of Goddess Kali. Would you like to go there to see the sacrifice of a black goat with suitable ritual, Sanjukta?'

There had been no possible answer to that, and Sanjukta had forced herself to meet his gaze calmly and with a faint touch of disdain that had aroused his admiration.

'What do you mean?' Sanjukta asked, stalling for time. She had an ugly and unpredictable temper and was altogether too autocratic and egotistical a woman to be relied upon to exercise patience and play a waiting game. There was a pregnant pause. His gaze rested upon her with possessive appreciation.

'Let's go,' interrupted Mr. Mitra wearily. They knew the underworld criminals would get through the maidan and the streets of the city in a threatening way to look for their victims at night. They knew those criminals had discolored the city's reputation unfairly. Racially prejudiced young people no longer felt they had a chance in society.

Holding her hand firmly, he got going with Sanjukta to the temple. As they got there, Mr. Mitra saw the light glint on the long blade of a knife, and the men nearest the priests and the brazier drew back and caught their breath in a harsh and simultaneous gasp that was clearly audible above the thudding beat of the drum. A priest came and cut the black goat's throat with suitable ritual. A shudder swept back through Mr. Mitra and Mrs. Sanjukta Das as a wave sweeps in from the sea, so that even those who could not see felt the surge of that savage emotion, and Mrs. Sanjukta was seized with a sudden sick horror, inexplicable and paralysing. A horror that crisped Mr. Mitra's hair and dried his mouth brought the cold sweat out on his forehead. He struggled to recover his old dignity. At this age he relied on his judgement.

Mr. Mitra was helplessly afraid with a fear that he had never known before. A primitive, primeval fear; not of death, but of evil.... He could hear the harsh the panting breath of the men about him, and it seemed to him as though they breathed as a pack of wolves might breathe; avidly, tongues lolling, circling about a wounded buck.

He heard her speak to a dozen people as they edged their way through the street, her voice light and gay. He noted as they passed that more than half the shops were closed and shuttered---sure sign of Muslim festival; that despite the intense heat the narrow stifling streets and alleyways were full of people as though it had been a fair day or a festival, and that the people talked in whispers and muttered in undertones.

Mr. Mitra left Mrs. Sanjukta abruptly at the turn into the wide stretch of local market. It was three hundred yards to go...two hundred...one hundred...fifty to reach the Old People's Home. He glanced at her and saw that she was angry, for her eyes shone and her bosom heaved.

He got back to Sanjukta. So, he sighed and kissed her, thereby setting the seal upon his shame and bondage. The boarders of their Old People's Homes were eagerly waiting for them. Sanjukta avidly said to him, looking at his worried-looking face, 'I'll have to wait for you at the same place by the tomorrow evening. Don't feel cheap. You must come without a fail. I know your old age remains one significant problem.' She was trying to prevent discovery of her checkered past. Mr. Mitra was silent and thinking about his age because he was unhappy and disappointed. He brushed aside his fears. Despite his old age, he still led an active life. He spun around to face Sanjukta.

She unbraided herself for the sentiment, but couldn't overcome or lessen it. Attempting to do so, she thought of those long-past days, when Mr. Mitra used to emerge at eventide from the seclusion of his study.

She went, leaving the vision of her glory to strive with the shame and sorrow in his heart. Mr. Mitra paused to peer into the gathering dusk, and in the silence he heard from somewhere far out across the darkening plains of maidan a dog barking at the evening star. He returned to Old People's Home. Every day was to him darker than the darkness of night.

It rained but poured. Over the flooded earth flew wind and darkness. All the stars were doused in ink-distended clouds. The worn-out street dogs sighed and moved their legs restlessly in darkness. Dead mice floated along the roads. Autumn set its ambushes about their hearts, and trees like naked corpses set upright on their feet swayed at the crossroads.

A hunch-backed elderly man was seen sitting beneath an age-old tree, staring straight ahead into nothingness. He remembered becoming very hungry and going out to a deserted area of maidan and taking out raw carrots to eat because he was afraid to disturb others.

He suffered the full impact of his wife's death but some of the laughter went out of his eyes and the bright bubble of wonder through which he had looked at the world before the death of his only son. Now he was alone.

Some morning walkers stood for long watching him. That hunch-backed elderly man turned and looked at the cradle which had been empty and waiting all those breathless months and where his wife slept quietly, the hiccoughs gone. And he went down to a nearby burial ground where his son had laid down. Looking at the gravestone, he got to feel: 'He who has no children doesn't know not what love is. Life is a continuous circle of death and killing. Why do we feel frightened at the time of death? As we grow in age, we will go in frustration. Why is Monday so far away from Friday but Friday is so close to Monday?' He cried out.

The trout ate the minnows—the hawk swooped on the mouse—half a dozen animals fed on their smaller neighbours. He heard the rabbit scream like a baby in the instant before its death—the only time in its life it ever made a sound as the agony of old persons. A new trouble was dawning on his thickening mental vision.

Chapter-III

As the cold wave of winter was gradually ebbing away, the age-old morning walkers felt that they would not work swiftly and methodically in the boiling sun of the summers. The sweat would pour off them and the dazzling glare of the river would scorch their faces and hurt their eyeballs.

Cooking was a difficulty on the pavements, for the pavement dwellers were afraid of showing smoke. In that still air it would have risen straight and betraying above the tree-tops, and they did not know who might see it. There were probably other fugitives living on the pavements, and the hunt might well be out against those who had taken refuge behind the Old People's Home. So they cooked only after dark or before dawn, and in the lower room of the ruin, blocking the door with a home-made curtain of grass and bamboo to avoid showing a gleam of light. It was a hot and choking performance, but Mr. Mitra and other boarders of Old People's Home managed it without complaint.

It had been morning when Mr. Mitra had awakened. A cold wet morning in which rain fell steadily and the doors creaked and shuddered and groaned. He could not forget Sanjukta. That appalling, agonising day had burnt itself into his brain. The early summer had been wet and cold, and the rain that had been falling as they drove to the Khidderpore docks had later given place to blustering gusts of wind that drove the dark banks of cloud before them and whipped the water of the river Ganges to a white froth of broken wave-tops.

Sanjukta lay still, remembering the details of yesterday's deplorable romance with horrified dismay. How could she have behaved so? Instead of insisting on decent privacy she had done nothing to prevent Mr. Mitra from

remaining silent about his leg amputated. A wild stab of anxiety hit Mr. Mitra. He got a cold, empty feeling in the pit of his stomach.

Mr. Mitra, lying flat on his stomach,, put down the empty cup of tea and muttered: 'The ladies have no attention to spare for anything but their own sufferings. A woman doesn't believe in permanence of love. I think a woman can safely stay there where she likes. Whereas man's a menace! A rumour-monger! ---Taken to nerves and the vapours like some melting female.' At that time the setting sun had thrown long and blue on the maidan, lay black behind him in the full blaze of the risen moon. These mental deceptions, however, came and went, nor did he ever mistake them for realities.

Once again Mr. Mitra paused to peer into the gathering dusk, and in the silence he heard from somewhere far out across the darkening plains slum children shouting at the evening star in a cheerful and ungrudging obedience to moonlight under the open sky. The sides of the nullah were steeper and narrower here than on the far side of the concealed entrance, and the dense bush arched above it and excluded the moonlight so that the place was almost as dark as the tunnel behind it. Then the darkness thinned. The track ran out into a clearing before the ruins of a long-forgotten fort or palace.

There was seldom much traffic on the roads in the heat of the day during the hot weather, and he passed an occasional lumbering bullock-cart, but nothing else. He had abandoned the pony by the roadside. He walked more hastily with the crutchs at first than was consistent with his strength; for a sort of guilty feeling, which sometimes torments men in their most justifiable acts, caused him to seek concealment from Sanjukta's eyes. Impelled by a wild and painful curiosity, he took a shelter at the earthy roots of an upturn tree, gazed earnestly at the desolate old man.

There was a smell of smoke in the hot air and a crackling sound, and emerging from the shelter of the oleanders Mr. Mitra saw that the slum house was on fire. He moved across the garden, leaving Mrs. Sanjukta standing alone in the open field. She looked everywhere but there was nothing to be found.

She was so exhausted from the day's journey that she went straight to bed. The mental horrors had always punished her of her father's undiscovered crime.

The morning sun was unclouded, and the trees and shrubs imbibed the sweet air of May; yet there seemed a gloom on Nature's face, as if she sympathised with mortal pain and sorrow of old persons lying asleep hither and thither under the open sky. Mr. Mitra's hands were uplifted in a fervent prayer. He felt Death would come like the slow approach of a corpse, stealing gradually towards him through the Old People's Home, and showing its ghastly and motionless features from behind a near and yet a near tree.

But such must have been his own fate if he had tarried another sunset. As he gave a parting look, a breeze waved the little banner upon the sapling tree and reminded him of his bow. During the several days, Mr. Mitra's recollection strayed drowsily among the perils and hardships through which he had passed, and he was incapable of returning definite answers to the inquiries with which many were eager to harass him. Mr. Sanjukta had detained him by captivity or by the stronger chain of death. Her selfish love of life had hurried him away before her father's fate. He got back to the Old People's Home with a heavy heart. He regretted, deeply and bitterly, the moral cowardice that had restrained his words when he was about to disclose the truth to Sanjukta.

In the calmest and clearest moods of his mind, his unburied romance was calling to his mind out of the wilderness. His one secret thought became like a chain binding down his spirit and like a serpent gnawing into his heart; and he was transformed into a sad and downcast yet irritable man. In bed he suddenly grasped for breath, his chest heaving. He tried stopping himself from falling down from the cot, gripping his pillow tightly. His heart stopped, working normally. He died in the wee hours of the morning in the midst of a rustle and a twitter of birds and the hoarse cawing of crows: the chatter of a squirrel and the creak of a well-wheel, and a conch blowing in a distant temple. His crutches were lying silently on his death-bed. It seemed to be crying making low, weak noises.

When death, like the sweet sleep which we welcome after a day of happiness, came over him, his far descendents would mourn over the venerated dust. As the boarders were informed of his death, they couldn't think clearly or speak. There was a stunned silence. There was a steady stream of elderly persons of other Old People's Homes. Some boarders studiously avoided answering the questions of others.

As Mrs. Sanjukta Das suddenly appeared in Old People's Home, his close friends looked at that elderly woman in disdain. Tears streamed down her face. Her answer was greeted with cries of anguish. She then paid her heart-felt respect to him and put a bouquet of attractive flowers at his feet. 'Pray Heaven,' said Mrs. Sanjukta in a broken voice, 'pray Heaven that neither of us dies solitary and lies unburied in this howling wilderness! She had a kind arm to hold his head and a kind voice to cheer in his last moments. O, death---the mystical experience of the Inner Light--- would have been awful to a solitary man in a wild place like Old People's Home!' Her mind wheeled around to the other extreme.

She hid her face in her robe, and even then, though her outstretched hand could touch the chill corpse of Mr. Mitra who had died cursing her. When the funeral rites had been performed, she would hence and cover herself from the eyes of his friends till those sorrows were forgotten. Now she felt the inner meaning of life. She uttered with a low inarticulate voice, looking at the sky:

'Life is like a beautiful and winding lane, on either side bright flowers, and beautiful butterflies, and tempting fruits, which we scarcely pause to admire and to taste, so eager are we to hasten to an opening which we imagine will be more beautiful still. By degrees as we advance, the trees grow bleak; the flowers and butterflies fall, the fruits disappear, and we find we have arrived.' She was then silently weeping in her room full of darkness. And she had blushed and shaken the wealth of grey hair from her ivory skin, and the soft lilting voice of her said: 'I am and I'm not. I have given answer to no one. Well, heaven forgive you, and all of us!'

The dark and gloomy pines of maidan looked down upon him as the wind swept through their tops, a pitying sound was heard in the maidan; or old trees groaned in fear that old persons were come to lay the axe to their roots at last. All the little incidental things and the big things, if there were any, disappeared.

www.ingramcontent.com/pod-product-compliance
Lightning Source LLC
LaVergne TN
LVHW010104170826
845678LV00012B/2239

* 9 7 9 8 8 4 7 5 4 2 8 6 9 *